SKY
EDGE

BY THE SAME AUTHOR

Splendor from the Sea
As a Tree Grows
Bold under God—A Fond Look at a Frontier Preacher
A Shepherd Looks at Psalm 23
A Layman Looks at the Lord's Prayer
Rabboni—Which Is to Say, Master
A Shepherd Looks at the Good Shepherd and His Sheep
A Gardener Looks at the Fruits of the Spirit
Mighty Man of Valor—Gideon
Mountain Splendor
Taming Tension
Expendable
Still Waters
A Child Looks at Psalm 23
Ocean Glory
Walking with God
On Wilderness Trails
Elijah—Prophet of Power
Salt for Society
A Layman Looks at the Lamb of God
Lessons from a Sheep Dog
Wonder o' the Wind
Joshua—Man of Fearless Faith
A Layman Looks at the Love of God
Sea Edge
David I
David II

SKY EDGE

W. Phillip Keller

Cover and Text
Illustrations by
Barbara Reed

WORD BOOKS
PUBLISHER
WACO, TEXAS

A DIVISION OF
WORD, INCORPORATED

Library of Congress Cataloging-in-Publication Data

Keller, W. Phillip (Weldon Phillip), 1920–
    Sky edge.

    1. Meditations.   I. Title.
BV4832.2.K416   1987   242   87–13298
ISBN 0–8499–3091–X

Printed in the United States of America
7898 RRD 987654321

In memory
of
Harvie
One of the finest companions
who
ever tramped a mountain trail
with me

Contents

A Note of Gratitude

This book has emerged from the agony and anguish shared with friends who faced great suffering and sorrow. For nearly two years we have tramped the trail of tears with various families who faced death with fortitude and faith. Only the presence of Christ could overcome the pain and pathos. To Him I give genuine gratitude for His grace and His strength to accomplish this work amid such adversity.

I am deeply thankful to my wife Ursula for sharing the sadness, even to tears, that brought this book to life. It is no light thing to enter fully into the suffering of others. Yet it is the noble service to which the Master calls us.

Lastly, the diligent art work done by Barbara Reed in preparing the pen-and-ink drawings is appreciated. Her hearty cooperation and energetic endeavors have been such a great help.

My Friend

He was tall and slim,
rugged as a cedar snag.
With great, strong hands,
quick to serve, ready to help
those of us in need.

He bore a gentle spirit,
free from guile or pomp.
His was a humble heart,
with a simple, quiet trust
in Christ our Living Lord.

We tramped the hills together.
We roamed the ridges free.
His eyes aglow with peace,
his face alight with fun,
for we were in his "realm."

He loved the lofty hills.
He loved the singing streams.
We shared their splendor often;
we revelled in their strength.
No need for more than these.

Enough to be his friend.

A tribute to Harvie Murfitt

1

The Birth of
This Book

This book, *Sky Edge,* is a collection of simple parables drawn from my adventures at the edge of the sky—on the high mountains I love so fiercely. It is intended as a companion piece to *Sea Edge,* written in the same style, produced in a similar format.

At the time *Sea Edge* was being created it was thought we would live by the ocean edge for the rest of our days. But it was not meant to be. Our Father had other plans for us. It became clear that we should return to the high, dry, vigorous climate of the interior, intermountain region of the west. So once again our "home terrain" was one of rolling rangeland nestled amid lofty mountain ranges that reached to the edge of the sky.

In His gracious, gentle way our Father had prepared a place for us. It is a cheerful, cozy, warm cedar chalet whose massive windows look out over a splendid landscape of rugged ranges, rolling hills and a small, shining mountain

lake. It is a very serene setting. Here we can hear the call of the Stellar Jays and the soaring hawks. At night the winsome wilderness call of the coyotes carries across the valley. We are surrounded with pines that sing in the wind, and shrubs of native origin that bear their own abundance of wild fruit.

A short, vigorous hike of only a few minutes takes me into terrain as primitive and untamed as it was when only the Indians hunted these hills. High snow-capped peaks stand on the perimeter of our mountain realm. Their melting snows feed sparkling streams. These in turn nurture mountain meadows and eventually shining lakes.

Within a radius of twelve miles of my front door can be found unspoiled mountain habitat that shelters bears, deer, mountain sheep, cougars, marmots, coyotes and a dozen other species of mammals. Here, too, is a variety of upland terrain that attracts scores of various bird species. Every sort of winged visitor spends part of the year in this upland realm, from the regal Golden Eagles that nest on our granite cliffs to the swift Barn Swallows that build beneath our eaves; from the great flocks of Canada Geese that nest in our lakes to the Mountain Bluebirds that adorn our high rangeland.

More than all of this, our high country is also a region of remarkable repose. Not that it is remote and inaccessible. That simply is not so. For not far away there are highways, towns, an airport and most of the other commercial activity that is characteristic of modern society. It just happens that where we live is a sheltered mountain valley that has remained almost untouched and untrammeled by modern man. And we feel fortunate indeed to savor its serenity for as long as our Father may desire.

In recent months I have relished mountain interludes of unusual uplift and inspiration. Never did I dream that such adventures would be mine so late in life. From the perspective of my advanced age they are doubly precious, both for their spiritual uplift, as well as their physical and mental stimulation.

This book is an earnest endeavor to share with the reader some of the stirring eternal truths which God, by His Spirit, has made so vivid and vital to me. He has always spoken to people of His choosing in the solitude of mountains. So it is appropriate that He should do so again.

It is not surprising that the Most High met with people like Noah, Abraham, Moses, Elijah and others in the high places. Even our Lord Jesus Christ often communed with His Father on the hill slopes and chose to reveal some of His greatest truths to His followers while on the mountains.

Like the sea, mountains often convey to us mortals the impression of immense durability. Yet they are subject to constant change. Weathering and erosion change their appearance. Still our Father uses them to speak emphatically to us earth children in flashes of spiritual insight.

Life in the high country can be most stimulating. The slopes challenge our strength, test our muscles, harden our bodies. The sweeping vistas and serene solitude energize our minds, quicken our souls and toughen our resolve. The grandeur and glory of the lofty peaks with star-studded skies sharpen our spirits and stir us to contemplate deeply the supreme issues of life.

It is in the quiet interludes on some remote ridge against the edge of the sky that God's eternal Spirit can speak with stunning clarity. There away from the crush and commotion of our culture He, Christ, God very God, can commune with us at great depths. In the stillness and solitude of the hills and valleys it is possible to know our Father and understand His eternal intentions for us.

Modern people, living amid the mayhem of our giant metropolitan centers, have been cut off from the wholesome benefits of the outdoor world. Most of modern life is so conditioned and shaped by the stresses and strains of a man-made environment that in many cases the healing influence of mountains, trees, streams, birds, fields and flowers is unknown and foreign to us. Perhaps this book can help reverse this tragic trend.

At the beginning of this introduction the assertion was made that our Father had certain specific reasons for bringing Ursula and me back to this mountain region. Unknown to us at that time was the responsibility of having our lives closely intertwined with families who faced terminal illness.

In just a little over a year we had, in a truly spiritual dimension, lived on the "sky edge" with fourteen families who faced death and all of its formidable consequences. Of these one was my own dearest friend, Harvie Murfitt, to whom this book has been dedicated. Up until six months ago he and I climbed, hiked and relished the high country together. Now he has gone on to even higher ground. He was a gracious, gentle, strong man. There are few like him around. How he is missed!

Besides him four others have crossed over the edge of the sky. And so it is that out of the deep sorrow, the intense suffering, the anguish of spirit that has been endured, some of the great principles explained here have been born. We have known in some small measure what Isaiah of old meant when he spoke of Christ as the One who bore our griefs and carried our sorrows.

This is not a shallow book designed just to entertain the reader. In parable form it deals with some of the most profound questions which confront us. The parables give sharp, clear glimpses into spiritual verities that transcend time and our few fleeting years upon the planet. They come to us bringing courage, consolation and serenity of soul.

My earnest hope is that through them our Father will give you bright light for the trail you tramp here. May He also give you sure and steadfast hope for life beyond the edge of the sky!

2

Four Bears and . . .

One mountain ridge I had often dreamed of climbing with Harvie lay just a few miles west of our home. It was typical of our high, dry, semidesert terrain. Like a long, slim mountain lion, crouched low against higher ranges, it bore the tawny color of sun-scorched grass, co-mingled with gray sage and rock. Scattered here and there were tough, old, wind-twisted firs and sturdy Ponderosa Pines that found footing in the stony soil.

It was always a thrill to tramp the new and strange game trails that criss-crossed the high country. And as I climbed slowly but steadily toward the clouds my spirit ached fiercely for the comradeship of my friend. How he used to take these hills in full stride! How his big, tall, raw-boned frame seemed designed to lift him easily over the tough terrain.

But Harvie was not here.

I was very much on my own—yet not alone!

For in a strange yet sure way, I sensed and knew the presence of God's Spirit accompanying me on the trail. Whatever His intentions, I was open to His touch—

receptive to any lesson He might wish me to learn in the dull overcast of that rainy day.

It was really a good day for a long, hard hike. The leaden sky and gentle drizzle cooled the late summer heat. The silver droplets of moisture clinging to every blade of grass and dry twig on the ground made for silent footfalls. So it was possible to pick up every sound that stirred in the soft silence of the lonesome hills.

As I topped the crest of the ridge I was startled to see it was cut off from the adjacent range by a deep, steep-walled canyon. On the far side sharp slopes of scree and broken rock rose sharply from the canyon floor.

Stopping to catch my breath, I stood in the shelter of a dense fir tree. Suddenly the sound of distant stones rolling down a slope caught my attention. Some sort of animal was on the move, loosening rocks that rumbled down into the canyon. All my senses were fully alert. What would it be?

Silently as the wraith of mist that swirled around me I moved along the rimrock of the canyon edge. I searched the opposite slopes for some sign of life, but could see nothing. Again there was the dull rumble of rolling rock. And once more I glided silently across the rain-softened ground. The whole world seemed so still, so serene, so at rest. Here was solitude of unusual intensity.

Through my binoculars I carefully scanned the rock slopes, shining with wetness. They seemed devoid of life until all at once my eyes caught the slight movement of the branches in a large serviceberry bush. Here we call them Olalla berries. In our upland world they often grow into massive shrubs up to fifteen feet tall and as many across.

A half-grown black bear, his coat glistening in the rain, was stripping the last of the summer fruit from the tall and slender branches. Within moments I found a second bear of similar size in another clump of brush, and then a third gathering the tender leaves from the tips of a hardy Vine Maple. Then as if to add a special delight to the day I discovered a fourth bear, a magnificent sow (female), obviously mother to the three younger ones, turning over rocks to find ants. It was she who had rolled the stones down the slopes.

Fortunately what feeble air currents were moving on the mountainside blew from the bears toward me. So it was possible to stalk them silently up my side of the deep defile until I was directly across the canyon from them. And now they were in full view.

What a rare and special treat this was! So often a man's encounter with wild bears is fleeting. Like dark shadows they slip away quietly into the trees and are lost to sight in a matter of moments.

How Harvie would have loved this interlude! How he revelled in watching wildlife! He would have grinned and chuckled with pure pleasure at such a show as this.

I spent the next four hours in constant company with those four beautiful bears. They were already heavy and rotund with the wild fruit that had flourished in such abundance during the summer. Their coats, black as a polished old coal stove, shone with health, vitality and well-being, now doubly so because of the mountain mist that sparkled on their fur.

The obvious gentleness and cordiality with which the four bears treated one another made an enormous impression on me. I had noticed and observed the same sort of behavior among elephants when I studied their family life years ago in Kenya.

There simply was no pushing or shoving or angry rivalry among them. I was especially surprised at how quiet and silent every move was, every gesture, every interaction between them. There appeared to be an aura of

23

courtesy and respect between the bears that warmed my own spirit in a strange yet wondrous way. If only human families were as cordial!

This was emphasized even further when I watched spellbound as one would actually bend over the branches of a bush and allow his companion to relish the fruit and leaves from it. Not once was there an outburst of anger or a hint of hostility.

Steadily but surely I stole closer and closer to the four until only about a hundred yards separated us. The old she-bear now decided it was time for an afternoon siesta. A giant, veteran fir had been blown down on the slope. It lay prostrate on the ground, a huge log now bare and stripped of bark. It would make a fine couch.

Here the four bears decided to stretch out and sleep away part of their afternoon. They curled up against each other, here a foreleg, there a hind leg, draped over one another's bodies. It was quite a scene and it surprised me none of them took umbrage at another for encroaching too close or shoving for the softest, smoothest spot.

I was being given a first-class object lesson in harmony of life. It appeared that utter peace and complete mutual understanding prevailed. There was no tension, no discord, no stress apparent.

After their siesta the four bears climbed down off the great gray log and began to forage for fruit and ants again. I began to call to them softly. The sound of my voice did not appear to disturb them. Rather, they seemed easily reconciled to my presence in their territory. It was a marvelous and touching finale to our time together.

I had been sitting quietly on a rugged, moss-covered outcropping of rock at the base of a gnarled tree that gave me shelter. As I stood up to leave I was startled by a huge mountain rattlesnake that had slipped up beside me unnoticed.

In swift, lightning-like action, he struck twice in rapid

succession. Fortunately I had on heavy bush pants and high-laced hiking boots. Still his sudden attack made every hair on my arms, legs and chest stand erect. He was aroused, alert and angry—perhaps even alarmed to see me stand up suddenly so tall beside him.

His rattles whirring with agitation he slithered into a dark crack in the rock that had been fractured by the roots of the old fir. I walked around it carefully. On the other side lay his shed skin. It stretched out just about four feet long, lying there shining on the stones. It had been a close call indeed. But through it I learned an unforgettable lesson.

In great seriousness I mused over the events of the day as I tramped the long trail home. I had been given a clear and vivid glimpse into one of the most profound yet powerful spiritual principles in life.

Things are not always as they appear!

This had been such a tranquil day. The mountains all draped in soft veils of mist, rain and moisture seemed so serene and still. Even the gentle interlude with the four bears gave one the feeling of quiet contentment and special pleasure.

Yet in the very midst of it all there lurked death. The rattlesnake was certainly the handsomest of his species I had ever seen. His thick, powerful body was adorned in striking bronze and black markings of special design.

Had his long fangs found their mark in my flesh, it is most likely it would have been a mortal wound. So large a charge of venom in one as old as I am could have meant death before I could tramp the long miles home.

It was a microcosm of life itself. For in the midst of our days, death is never really far removed. At almost any hour, from some unexpected quarter, the last and final call may come swiftly and in a most surprising way. We never can tell when the fatal moment will appear.

So the serious, sobering questions must be asked:

"Do I live ready to die?
Is my life in order?
Do I know and love God as my Father?
Is Christ my closest friend?
Is all well between me and others?"

Just a few months before this incident Harvie and I had made a late winter climb together. It had been such a joyous adventure, filled with fun and good cheer.

I recall so clearly how we scaled the last ridge all shining with deep snow. There in a sheltered spot we shared our sandwiches and tea while the sparkling midday sun warmed our faces and hands. Never, never, never did either of us dream that terminal cancer would soon snatch him away. Death stalked the dear fellow that day and we did not know it.

So, things are not always as they may appear. And the only guarantee we can have not to be taken unaware is to have made our peace with God through the great generosity of the wondrous, amazing grace of Christ. Then the call home can come at any moment. And all is well!

The second startling insight which God's gracious Spirit imprinted upon my own spirit that day was this: *Even in the most harmonious settings, the enemy of our souls is at hand to disturb.*

As God's people we sometimes delude ourselves into believing that we can live lives of serenity here on earth without fear of attack from the evil one. It simply is not so. Satan appeared in paradise to disrupt the sublime arrangements made for Adam and Eve. He appeared in the desert to assail our Lord and Master Jesus Christ in His great enterprise for our salvation. So he is bound to bother us.

The serpent is not a figment of man's imagination. He is not some superstitious fabrication of ancient folklore. A deadly foe opposed to all that is fine and noble and upright in the earth, he is the implacable enemy of God and His people. He insists on insinuating himself into the most harmonious of our situations. He poses a perilous threat even in the most sanguine of our days. He is swift to move and ready to attack in the most unlikely moments.

It is for this reason that the Spirit of God alerts us again and again to be on our guard against the evil one. Even our Lord, with enormous understanding, taught us to pray daily: *"Our Father who art in heaven . . . . deliver us from evil"* (or the evil one).

Fortunately for me, long years of wilderness experience had taught me the basic behavior essential to survival in the high country. One went properly attired in heavy bush pants, high-laced hiking boots, warm clothing and, above all, with alert senses. Reflexes must be swift and smooth and silent.

So it is, too, in the Christian experience. Our walk with God through the tangled trails of this brief earthly sojourn is not without its perils. There are abroad in the wilderness of our days not only high adventures with Christ but also some severe risks. The Word of God alerts us to these.

In passages such as the sixth chapter of Ephesians we are given explicit instructions as to what antagonists we can and will encounter. We are supplied with specific information on how to equip and garb ourselves so that we can survive unexpected emergencies.

Sometimes we are startled by the sudden appearance of the enemy, no matter what guise he assumes. But this does not mean we need to fall prey to his devices. If we are properly equipped in soul and spirit against his attack it will come to nothing. When we are fully alert with the Word of God active in our lives, we survive unscathed.

These are precautions we must take as Christians. There need not be disaster even if there is great danger abroad. Provision is made for our overcoming the evil one if we will calmly obey our Master's instructions and quietly carry out His directions for our lives.

He will lead us in paths of righteousness and peace. But we must allow Him to be our constant companion on the trails of life.

3

The Beauty of Bunch Grass

In our lofty landscapes, where the mountains push their ragged ridges against the edge of the sky, one of the most common scenes is a swath of golden grass, spread like a tufted blanket between the trees. For only a few weeks in early spring does this golden glory appear as a faint mantle of tender green.

The clear, clean, sun-drenched atmosphere of the high country quickly turns the bunch grass slopes to burnished bronze. Ours is essentially a rangeland of sun-bleached golden grass with dark and handsome trees scattered across it to give the impression of open parkland.

This is the region where fine herds of cattle graze the summer range. Deer abound and the mountain winds blow softly, whispering among the trees, bending the grass like waves of flowing gold. It is glorious country in which to hike or ride a horse. A realm of long views and wide expanses, its high horizons challenge the spirit and call to the wild, free emotions of a mountain man.

Some of my most memorable years have been spent in this rugged mountain world. At one time I owned nearly a thousand acres in one of the upland valleys. There was an ancient log cabin there, perched beside a tiny stream that tumbled over the cliffs into a lake nearby. I wrote seven books in the rough shelter of that thick-walled cabin—books filled with beautiful photos and passionate cries for the preservation of all things wild. They had such titles as *Under Wilderness Skies* and *Under Desert Skies*. Their basic uplift and inspiration were born in the thrilling atmosphere of the high bunch grass ranges.

Our native bunch grass has been called one of the most noble living plants upon the planet. Some ecologists consider it to be the supreme species of grass in North America. Other specialists call it "the great healer." This is because of the remarkable benefits it bestows on the land.

To those who generally think of grass as a smooth green lawn, closely clipped and meticulously manicured by man, our native mountain variety comes as a rough, tough surprise. It grows in sturdy clumps, really like a tussock of tough stems intertwined with slender leaves that can feel rough to the touch.

Each tussock is separated from its fellows by bare soil or open ground. This space between the bunches of grass is often shaded by the tall stems of the seed heads which in good grass country may be two or three feet tall. Seldom is the stand of grass so dense or thick as to form a solid mat. Rather, it appears like an old-fashioned tufted rug flung casually across the countryside. Each bunch of tough plant fibers glows gold against the dark underlayer of the land itself.

This covering of grass will and can grow on stony slopes so steep that they are almost vertical. It is so sturdy, so deep rooted, so tenacious it can thrive on thin soils where other plants succumb. Despite blazing summer days when heat in these hot hills pushes well above 100° F it still flourishes under the burning skies. Where wind and weather and trampling hooves and human abuse would wipe out any other grass, this hardy species still survives. The secret lies in its tremendous root system.

A single clump of bunch grass may have miles of hairlike underground roots that reach out to tap the hidden nutrients in the soil. Each plant sends out an intricate network of rootlets that not only anchor it to the slopes but draw life, moisture and sustenance from the mountain terrain.

So deep, so far reaching, so extensive is the bunch grass root system that intensive scientific studies have shown a single plant to have up to seventeen miles of rugged roots! Little wonder this sturdy species can withstand so much grazing, so much trampling, so much abuse from reckless ranchers who often overgraze the range.

Year after year the bunch grass patiently puts out new growth. Season after season it sends up fresh shoots to shimmer in the sun. Generation after generation its golden glory cloaks the high country to gladden our spirits and nourish all those who rely on it for sustenance.

Cattle come down off the bountiful bunch grass ranges in fall, so fat, so well nourished that they appear to have been stall-fed on grain. The rich protein content of the grass is some of the finest forage in all the world. Even when it is bleached and glowing bronze it bears within its fibers a level of nutrition seldom matched by any other plant material.

When winter storms blanket the ranges in snow, deer and mountain sheep and range horses will seek out the open, southwest slopes to feed on the sturdy bunch grass clumps. The tough fibers, so rich in protein, like well-cured hay, will fuel their inner fires fighting off the chilling cold.

Yes, in spring, summer, fall and even in winter, bunch grass is beautiful. It is the gentle healer of the hills, the

sustainer of life, the golden carpet flung so freely over the land by our Father's generous care.

Several days ago the dawn broke calm and clear and cloudless. It was a typical late summer morning in our mountain valley. The golden light of the sun's low rays stretched softly across the tawny bunch grass hills that partially fill the views from our wide front windows. The warm glow of the open range was like an eager invitation to go out and climb the ridges. So I responded at once.

Happily for me, the areas adjacent to our home are some of the choicest bunch grass country I have ever known. For one reason and another they have not been abused, burned, overgrazed or even trampled too much. These bunch grass hills are still in a pristine state of natural splendor seldom seen.

Droplets of moisture clung to the clumps of grass as I climbed the steep rock ridges above our house. The dense tufts, now heavy with their annual seed heads, carpeted the steep slopes in beautiful bronze shades. As I broke out over the summit I came across fresh deer tracks where a band of Mule Deer had been feeding in the dawn.

Then suddenly I stepped from the shaded side of the rock ridge into the full glory of the morning sun on the south side. The scene made me stand in awe, stunned by the exquisite beauty of the bunch grass. Never had I seen it in quite such an enchanting light.

The low slanting rays of the rising sun ran almost parallel with the slope. The soft light touched each individual tussock so that it glowed from within. It was as if ten million lamps strewn at random across the undulating range had suddenly been lit, each with a living flame of golden inner fire. It was one of those sublime, passing, precious moments in time, etched forever on the memory.

And in that instant of time my spirit was touched deeply!

As I stood in silence the questions came swiftly.

The gracious Spirit of the living God was dealing with my soul in profound intensity.

Did this little life of mine, lived out quietly on the edge of the sky, in any way remotely resemble bunch grass?

Was there anything beautiful about it, even if it seemed so very ordinary?

Could it be said of me that I was one who brought healing to these hills, help to those around me?

Did my presence in this place contribute to the well-being and nourishment of those who in quiet trust turned to me for sustenance?

Were the roots of my being so deeply driven into the very life of the living Christ that there I found the ground of my being?

Was it the very vitality of His vigorous life that sustained me amid all the vicissitudes of my experiences?

Could my Master say of me with calm approval that in season, out of season, my days had been a delight to Him, a benediction to His people, a benefit to my generation?

Despite the reverses of life; despite the heat of the day; despite the trampling of others; despite the carelessness of my contemporaries—did I still quietly put on new growth year after year?

Was I rich forage for famished people?

In times of stress and distress did someone here find sustenance to sustain them in their strain?

Were there those moments in time when my life glowed, touched and transformed by the warm light and gracious love of God, my Father?

I came down off that mountain deep in reflection, moved by those still moments of meditation. A rough mountain man had been touched by the Most High!

4

Mountain Climbing

At the age of fifteen I climbed my first major mountain. It was Mount Kilimanjaro on the border between Kenya and Tanzania in East Africa. The blood-tingling thrill of setting one's feet on high ground, against the edge of the sky, ignited a flame of enthusiasm for the high country then that has never left me.

Since that first mountain adventure, well over fifty years past, I have climbed ranges scattered throughout various regions of the world. Perhaps it is the wild, free spirit of my Swiss forebears that has produced such a passion within me for the high places. Still it is there. And though I am now well advanced in years, the lure of the peaks still grips me fiercely, constraining me again and again to respond to the challenge of the upward trail.

Above and beyond the adventure of getting onto higher ground, there lies deep within my being an intimate love for rugged hills, upthrust alp-lands and the splendor of shining snowfields that crown the summits. Unlike many climbers who see this realm as a mere fortress of rock, ice and snow to be beaten by brute strength, climbing skill and

41

special rock techniques, I view it as a magnificent environment in which to move and live with awe and wonder.

I have written much about this in some of my previous books such as *Canada's Wild Glory* and *Mountain Splendor*. Both by word pictures and beautiful photographs an attempt has been made to share with the readers some of the majestic wonders of the high mountain realms I have explored.

But here I am concerned with the actual exercise of climbing followed by its immediate benefits to the climber. In short—what it means to climb!

Hiking in high-country places puts a certain strenuous demand upon one's strength and stamina. It is not a gentle stroll in the park. It calls for fortitude, for discipline of mind and muscle, for vigor of spirit to push toward the summit.

Often the climb begins with a rather tedious trail at the foot of the mountain. This leads through thick timber, windfalls and steep switchbacks where only here and there a distant glimpse of peaks encourages one to press on.

Bit by bit the trees begin to thin out. With increasing altitude the timber becomes more stunted, broken and beaten down by wind, snow and fierce ice storms. Here, too, the air becomes thinner, less charged with oxygen. Vistas widen, distant views quicken the pulse and the air is pungent with the perfume of pine, fir and spruce.

Then the trail breaks out above tree line. Sweeping alpine meadows of short grass, lowly heather, glowing wildflowers and broken rock beckon the climber to move higher. Here is the sky edge. This is where heaven seems to touch earth. It is a realm as yet unravaged or ruined by the hands of man.

Finally, for the hardiest of climbers there stands the summit. All sheathed in ice, snow and giant rock buttresses, its peaks comb the clouds, or, if the weather is clear, stand stark and beautiful against a brilliant blue sky.

It is a world of great stillness, punctuated only by the undulating sounds of a distant waterfall, a whistling marmot or the lone cry of an eagle. It is a realm of incredible grandeur and glory. Fields, aglow with millions of multi-hued wildflowers, stretch up to the ridges. Vast, wide valleys sweep away to the horizon. Mountain lakes sparkle in the sun. And all around lies co-mingled snow and sky and stone.

There is a stimulation, an uplift, an all-engulfing enthusiasm which energizes the soul in such a setting. The person who has spent time at the edge of the sky is never, ever, quite the same again. He or she has tasted the thrill of the lofty landscapes and learned to love them through intimate, personal contact.

This was especially true of my friend Harvie. His favorite mountain realm was "The Cathedrals," a rugged range lying about forty miles west of our homes. The first time I climbed there it impressed me so profoundly I immediately petitioned the Provincial Government to set the region aside as a park. In due time, by sheer patience and perseverance, this came about. So today it is one of the finest wilderness preserves in British Columbia.

Here was where Harvie loved to climb. This is where he went again and again for renewal of body and strong invigoration of spirit. And it is there where his ashes have been buried amid the splendors of the upland meadows he loved so dearly.

We often hiked in the foothills of that range together, even in mid-winter when snow blanketed the slopes and ice had locked the rushing rivers in its blue embrace. Still we would hike there to watch the deer, to see the wild sheep, to find the mountain goats on their cliffs—but most important just to be together in the high country.

From long experience we had learned to set a calm, steady, even pace. We did not try to rush the slopes in a sudden burst of energy. Often we paused, but only briefly to catch our breath, to rest our muscles, to renew our vigor. We took time to study the birds we met, to read the wildlife tracks along the trail, to relish the ever-widening views. We would stop to sit in the sun and enjoy a sandwich, a cup of tea or a jovial chat. There would be creeks to cross, rocks to climb and windfalls to get over. But it was all mountain climbing. So we took it in stride and loved it all.

Getting onto "higher ground" with God is much the same. There are too many Christians who seem sure they can attain the summit of spiritual experience with a single startling surge of energy. It is almost as if they thought the lofty life of communing with Christ could be achieved with one bold leap of faith, or some single session at a weekend retreat.

This simply is not so.

Our Father invites us to walk with Him steadily and surely, day by day, taking one step of faith after another in calm succession. There will be interludes in which the trail may seem very tedious. It may even appear to go up, then down, back and forth, in rather boring switchbacks. There will be times when nothing thrilling excites our view. Yet we can still be gaining ground.

As we go on with God we are bound to encounter some windfalls and downed timber as well as rushing creeks of misfortune. There are going to be obstacles to surmount, deep waters to ford, before we get out of the woods. Christ never guaranteed that the going would all be easy.

Even when we do break out into the open alpine meadows above timber line there will be miry stretches along the trail. The chill, upland atmosphere can cut to one's bones. The experience of wide horizons and awesome vistas can be tempered by biting winds and driving sleet. It is worth them all.

When we keep company with Christ in the lofty life of

separation from the common crowd, we find there is a high cost. That cost is one of accepting the challenge daily to do His will and comply with His wishes. It might seem much easier just to settle down in a soft spot. It may entail the criticism of others around us.

But He calls us to push on with Him steadily. Our Lord wants us to take the upward view of the sky edge. He calls us to live dangerously with Him in the full and abundant joy of His hearty companionship in the high country.

Yesterday was a classic example of this principle. The day broke dull with a gray, leaden sky hanging low over the hills. A raw wind, with ice on its breath, blew down the slopes from the first heavy snowfall of the autumn season that decorated the ridge tops.

It would have been so easy, so comfortable, so pleasant just to lay a crackling fire in the hearth; to draw up my favorite reading chair by the laughing flames; to settle down and enjoy an engrossing book, then, with Puma (our cat) lying on my lap, while away the morning in luxurious ease.

But the call of the mountain trail was insistent.

The challenge to go out into the high country was clear.

The cost of climbing was considered and accepted.

Quietly I slipped into long winter underwear. The sturdy boots for mountain climbing were laced securely. A heavy wool shirt that has taken me through a hundred storms was buttoned over my chest. A well-worn windbreaker and snug wool cap completed my attire. Then I was off for the hills.

The chill wind made my lungs ache. The steep trail put a fierce strain on my legs and thighs. They cried for relief. But I pushed on steadily. I was determined to scale the ridge to reach the summit of a range I had never been on before.

That is really what the challenge of Christian life on

high ground is like. It is a series of choices. Am I going to accept the challenge, count the cost and move out of my comfortable lifestyle to tramp the trail of testing and self-discipline with Him? Am I willing to be "wrung out," exposed to hardship and exercised to the limit to gain ground with God?

Do I truly love Him with all my mind, soul, strength and heart as I love the sky edge?

"To truly love God with all one's heart" is perhaps the most maligned and least understood phrase in the church today. Its counterpart, "and love your neighbor as yourself," is equally obscure and distorted by our soft society.

From God's perspective, "to love" is to entertain and express good will toward another. It is to set the will to seek the best for all concerned. It is abandoning every element of selfish self-indulgence to expend one's self fully for the well-being of all others.

This is the high calling to which Christ calls His followers. Not until we walk this noble way do we know anything of living the lofty life to which He summons us. There is a high cost to it. It is not the soft, sensual sentiments of people who are pursuing an "emotional high" assuming it to be the quintessence of spiritual experience.

As I climbed yesterday this truth came home to me with a clarity as sharp, cutting and acutely defined as the biting wind that cut across my cheeks and numbed my hands.

No, mountain climbing is not a stroll in the park. It is not always a saunter in the warm sunshine of a spring day. It can be a tough ordeal in which a man must face sleet and rain, cold or heat, snow-laden skies and sometimes blue skies. He has to be prepared and ready for any weather.

As I broke out above the clouds, a soft, subdued glow of Indian summer sunshine enveloped the open mountain meadows. Its warm light touched the flaming Vine Maples, igniting them with its glory. It lit up the burnished coat of a magnificent Mule Deer that bounded up the slope. It glistened from the wings of a skein of geese gliding across the sky edge.

It had been worth climbing the challenging heights.

I basked in the sun at the crest of the ridge. All was well!

For a few moments I snuggled down into the silver sage that grew on the summit of the range I had climbed. It had been touched by frost. Its pungent aroma permeated the clean, crisp mountain atmosphere. It was pure delight to inhale its fragrance, to sense the stimulation of its uplifting perfume.

This was the essence of the sweeping upland range. It was the exhilaration of the sky edge where the mountains met the sky. This wild, free, upland realm was where eagles rode the thermals and Meadowlarks sang in the sage.

Rare interludes like this are precious moments a man can store in the vault of his memory. They are beautiful bonuses given from my Father's generous hand. They are gifts of pure pleasure bestowed by His bounty.

But they would never have been mine had I chosen instead just to sit softly by my hearth. They would have been missed had I preferred just to stay at home, refusing to risk the storm or tackle the trail.

Contentedly I gazed out across the sweeping panorama of upland valleys and upthrust ranges that lay stretched out beneath me like a giant relief map. I could see more than fifty miles from my high vantage point. The whole world lay still, subdued, wrapped in the faint blue haze so typical of early autumn.

Only the distant cry of the wild geese at the very edge of the sky drifted down to the lone man high on the hill.

But I was not alone, for God very God, by His Spirit was present in that splendid mountain sanctuary.

Sharing the interlude with me, He had quickened my spirit. He had stirred my soul to the depths.

With joyous stride I headed home down the slopes, plunging through the clumps of bunch grass and broken rocks. On the way I gathered a bundle of flaming maple leaves to decorate the hearth at home.

It was a triumphant farewell to a splendid mountain climb.

5

Eagles in the Wind

The afternoon was wrapped in September sunshine. Warm air filled the river valley below the cliff on which I sat. From my lookout I could scan the ranges that stretched away into blue smudges on the farthest horizon. This was immense country over which eagles could circle wide in the air against a backdrop of cumulus clouds.

Lost in the luxury of the day's deep contentment, I lay on my back watching the drifting clouds. The fragrance of the tender grass pressed beneath my body scented the air, mingling with the piney aroma of sap oozing from the branches of the craggy old snag beside me.

I knew this particular tree was a favorite perch for the eagles. Long ago its majestic crown had been broken beneath the blast of a brutal ice storm. The shattered limbs, twisted and torn from their sockets in the trunk, dangled in dejection from the proud old tree, growing gray and hard as bone with years of wind and weather. Near the base of the tree a fragment of daring greenery still survived. Here the sap still struggled in spring to push out a spray of new needles and fresh cones from its stubby, twisted branches.

Despite its broken crown, one sturdy old limb stood defiant in death, like an upthrust arm with knotted muscles against the stern sky. Here the eagles sat and scanned the valley below. Patiently they came to wait for the rising warm air currents that would lift them high above the rock ridges of their wild realm. Here they sat and screeched their high-pitched cries that slanted down across the rock cliffs below them.

So I lay there on this dreamy day, a grass stem between my teeth, my head propped on a gnarled root for a pillow. But as the afternoon passed into evening I found I was not alone. High above my head two tiny specks, scarcely visible to my naked eyes, cut long spirals against the clouds. It was a pair of eagles, and I watched them circle slowly toward their tree where they would wait out the night.

The beautiful scene from Isaiah 40:31 leaped into my mind: "They that wait upon the Lord shall renew their strength; they shall mount up with wings as eagles; they shall run, and not be weary; and they shall walk, and not faint."

Entranced with the eloquent language, so simple yet so descriptive, I watched the great birds soaring on the warm air currents. Slowly there penetrated my mind and heart an acute appreciation of the precise picture that the grand old prophet, Isaiah, was trying to portray to his discouraged people. Most of his audience were simple country folk who, if they had never seen eagles, at least were familiar with the kites and vultures that are so prominent a part of rural life in the Middle East.

But for me on this summer day these two birds soaring majestically over their wilderness domain were the pristine picture of the Christian as a conqueror.

"They that wait upon the Lord shall renew their

strength . . . ." The words kept running through my mind time and time again. Waiting—wasn't this precisely what I had watched eagles doing so often—just sitting, resting, waiting?

All through the darkest nights, through the cold, gray gloom of morning the birds simply rested patiently, renewing their strength, waiting, perched on some dead snag or crag of rock.

The eagles know from experience that as the sunshine floods the valleys and warms the rocks and earth, gentle updrafts of air will start to rise above the surrounding ridges. It is on these thermal currents that they will soon soar with ease.

So they sit quietly, not fretting or worrying about whether they will be taken aloft. They know they will be. They renew their strength while they wait.

This is the picture of a Christian passing through the dark hours of danger and discouragement. All around him he can sense the chill downdrafts of frustration and reverses. It seems God's face is hidden from him and he cannot see ahead. Yet he need not be despondent. Rather, this is the time to wait for the Lord, to rest in the confidence that He is true to Himself in utter faithfulness.

Then it is that the first rays of morning sunshine reach the crest of the cliff and touch the eagle's feathers. He shakes himself, fluffs his plumage and with new interest watches the valley below him fill with golden light. Since he knew this would happen, his calm waiting has restored his strength and renewed his vigor.

At first, almost imperceptibly, but growing ever stronger, he feels the warm air currents rising around him, lifting gently from the valley floor past his perch.

Presently the regal bird spreads his wings and launches himself confidently into space. At once the thermal currents are bearing up beneath his wings and he rides them splendidly. By deliberate effort the eagle keeps himself in the center of the updrafts, rising higher and higher, borne aloft, mounting ever upward until he is lost to sight.

What a sublime etching this is of the Christian in his relationship to God. On the outstretched wings of prayer and praise he launches himself out upon the promises of God, depending on the great updrafts of His faithfulness to bear him up.

It takes courage to do this. A daring act of faith is required for us to let go of the limb to which we have clung for so long and launch ourselves fearlessly into the great open space before us.

As the bird by the discipline of keeping his wings outstretched to catch every eddy of air mounts up with ease, so the Christian, if he would overcome, must school himself continually to spread his heart before God in an attitude of never-ceasing prayer and praise, looking to Christ.

The updrafts of God's faithfulness are forever. It is up to us to rest upon that faithfulness. This we can do only by holding ourselves in the center of His purpose through a deliberate and continuous attitude of prayer and praise.

Probably the thing that impresses anyone who has watched eagles soaring the most is the apparent ease and utter serenity with which they fly. Of course this would be impossible without the skill that comes from long practice.

The demands made upon the Christian who would lead a triumphant and serene life are no less exacting. The young believer will often grow weary. He or she will be tempted to relax vigilance. One will be impulsive and prone to a faltering up-and-down experience. Like a young eagle, one will do a good deal of flapping and flopping around before he or she has mastered the art of continuous soaring. In fact, one might become quite exhausted and downcast on occasion from trying so hard to fly on one's own strength instead of just resting on God's faithfulness.

All these thoughts poured through my heart on that warm day. Evening was settling over the ridges, and I watched the proud birds circling slowly down toward the tree where I sat.

For them darkness was approaching, and in the cool of the night they would rest and wait upon the gnarled branch of the old pine, renewing the strength that had been spent in keeping their wings outstretched all day.

With the rising of the sun tomorrow they would mount up on fresh wings.

The glorious flight of the regal birds is not always without adversity. Eagles, too, have times when they are tested and tormented by rowdy attacks from lesser birds.

One day, hiking in the hills west of my cottage, I was astonished to see a mob of crows pursuing an eagle at treetop level. The daring "black jacks" would dive down on the beleaguered bird in angry attacks. Crow after crow hurtled down on the eagle like black bombers bent on destruction.

Though the great bird twisted and turned in mid-flight, lashing out in self-defense with sharp talons and rapier beak, he was no match for the infuriated mob of black bandits. They were doing their best to drive the regal eagle into the timber.

Suddenly, to my unbounded surprise, the great bird swooped up to a giant old snag that stood etched against the sky on a granite cliff. In a split second he had settled securely on a gnarled limb. He shook out his ruffled feathers, adjusted his strong stance, then peered about him with piercing eyes.

Instantly the crows called off their attack. As if by a supersensitive signal every one of the daring black acrobats peeled off from the attack to fly away in disarray. The monarch of the air was supreme where he stood, waiting calmly for any crow foolish enough to come within reach of his flashing, swordlike bill.

Standing there on the ancient, twisted tree, the eagle was again at ease. Every movement of his magnificent head and glowing eyes spoke of strength, assurance, power and prestige. He was waiting, ready for the worst that never came. He was in control again.

The eagle had shown that he was more than a match for any mob of crows trying to gang up on him. He was able to meet their attack and master their daring devices. But to do so he had long ago discovered he could do it best by simply waiting quietly in strength.

There was a most profound lesson for me in that brief episode that afternoon. The best of believers have those moments in life when suddenly they feel mobbed and harried by either adverse circumstances that suddenly arise on the horizon, or the cruel attacks of their contemporaries.

One simply cannot get through life without excruciating experiences of this kind. It is absolutely inevitable that there will be days when it seems we are going to be driven into destruction. People or events just do gang up on us. The irony of life is that calamities, like the crows, come in bunches of unexpected, rapid sequence, one rushing in upon another.

Often our first impulse is to flee or take flight. Somehow we want to take to the trees. We lash out left and right hoping to keep the destruction at bay. But we seldom succeed.

The more prudent move is to settle down in stillness, waiting quietly for the crisis to pass. This is not an easy decision to make. It often seems much more heroic to try to fight our way out of the fray. Yet that is not the best way.

The longer I live, the more often I discover that to wait patiently is the secret to power and peace. Standing quietly, serene in the strength that comes from knowing Christ, one can overcome. Wait upon the Most High. Trust in His remarkable wisdom. Let the strength of His Spirit support us. All will be well!

6

Snow-fed Streams

Clear, cold, pure water pouring out of the high country in constant, abundant supply is one of the exhilarating joys of the sky edge. Singing streams, tumbling waterfalls, roaring rivers all rumbling down their valleys are as eternal as the snowfields that comprise their source.

As long as winter and summer, springtime and autumn move majestically across the mountains, so will the snow-fed streams refresh the hills and nourish the valleys below. In the flowing water there is life and power and renewal for the earth.

In our rugged northern ranges the snow and rain have their origin in the uncharted, windswept reaches of the vast north Pacific. From out of the immensity of the ocean depths great winds pick up their burden of moisture and carry it aloft across the coast to set it down upon our western slopes. There in giant drifts of snow, some eighty feet deep, the precious moisture seeps into the soil and percolates gently into bubbling springs and melting freshets.

Ultimately, after weeks and months of travel down

the mighty mountain valleys, the water returns again to the sea whence it came. The cycle is completed. The water has run its course. And there it lies again, ready to be borne aloft and carried over the land.

This powerful process is as ancient as the earth itself. It is as eternal as the tides. It is as enduring as the rock over which the water runs. All of these are relative aspects of a planet which had a specific beginning in time and will come to a significant end in future. But for the brief duration of our earth days it appears to us to be everlasting.

This is why poets, philosophers and mystics have always turned to the eternal hills for uplift and inspiration. It is why they have sought the solace of the sea in their soliloquies. It is why they have written and sung of flowing streams and deep-running rivers.

Instinctively man's soul seeks that which endures. His spirit yearns for something no longer transient but eternal. His innermost being longs to be identified with the everlasting, for in truth his spirit is indestructible.

Often, without shame or embarrassment, I have turned to the sky edge with its tumbling streams and melodious sounds to find solace for my soul, healing for my heart. There comes gentle strength and quiet assurance in the acute awareness that these upper springs have flowed undiminished, unchanged for ten thousand years. There can be renewal here at the edge of a snow-fed stream that flows from the rock with pristine purity as clean as the wind-driven snow on the summit.

Again and again, in a long lifetime of wilderness trails and testing mountain climbs, I have stooped to bury my face in the swift running rivulets of an upland stream. Long and deeply have I drunk of its cold delicious fluid. I have been refreshed, renewed, ready to push on again with the heavy pack on my back.

Besides the physical refreshment of a snow-fed

stream, there is a unique and special quality to the music it makes: the murmuring of its soft flow between the stones; the muted tones of its gentle laugh as it tumbles over ledges of rock; its low rumble when it rolls the boulders in its bed in full flood. Depending on the mountain breezes, these sounds rise and fall with constant variations as if played by a celestial orchestra.

Yes, there is music in the mountains. There is uplift for the weary soul. Rejuvenation awaits the spirit ready to listen and be refreshed. This is music of divine origin. Its melodies caressed the creation long before man set foot on the scene. Its harmony can heal in wondrous ways. There is deep and profound therapy in the flow of water, in the songs of a stream.

Modern man, far removed from the natural balm of such a serene source of inspiration, is only just beginning to rediscover the wonders of running water. Creeping shyly out of the grim ghettos of their own building, a few are seeking solace at the sky edge where streams still run clear.

But we mountaineers have always known that there was help and healing in the high country. We have turned our tired feet toward the upward trails. We have found peace and rest and splendid strength in the streams that were suckled by the shining snow.

This was true for me when Harvie passed over "the great divide." When the final tribute had been paid to this splendid man, I turned to the high mountains and sought solace beside a rushing stream that carved a mighty channel through the untamed wilderness.

I needed desperately to be reassured that life could still go on flowing in strength as did this fine river. I needed to hear the pulsing, profound music that had endured an eternity and could be composed just as surely in my own agonizing soul. I needed to sense the power, the purity, the life, the potency that flowed from above.

My Father did not disappoint me. In the serenity and strength of that stream He spoke to me emphatically. He touched me in unmistakable terms.

It was a warm summer afternoon when I made camp near the stream. The heavy pungency of hemlock and fir needles, stressed by the sun, hung in the air. Underfoot a deep carpet of needles and cones cushioned my footfalls. Chipmunks scurried through the underbrush. And in the distance there played the soft music of the stream, its melodies drifting through the trees. It invited me to draw near, to listen to its song and drink of its coolness.

Taking a thick terry towel and my well-worn Testament, I started down the trail to the stream bank. Deer, bears and coyotes had made a well-used trail down to the water's edge. It ran over ancient, gnarled roots of poplars, pines and dense cedar thickets. Gently I worked my way along the stream until I found a giant slab of stone that jutted out into the swiftly moving current.

Here I spread my towel on the sun-warmed rock and stretched myself beside the singing waters. I was opening my soul to any message the stream might bring to me from my Father's great heart of compassion. Crushed with the departure of one I held so dear, I needed healing and restoration.

The first powerful impression that swept into my soul was the incredible clarity and pristine purity of the water pouring over the rocks all around me. The fluid was utterly transparent, so free of any contamination that I could see every pebble, every stone, every grain of sand in the stream bed.

This was virgin snow water, as cold as ice, as clear as the finest crystal. It surged down the valley cleansing, refreshing, stimulating every life form it touched.

"Exactly like the life of God!" I mused to myself. "The life that comes flowing to me from the eternal Christ is utterly pure—free of any pollution. It carries no silt, no mud, no debris, no contamination into the complexity of our earth days!"

With sudden, startling insight I realized that just as I had drawn near to this stream to drink deeply of its freshness, to plunge my face into its cooling depths, so Christ had invited me to come to Him and drink deeply of His invigorating, ever-abundant life. The source was inexhaustible, the supply ever new, the flow unceasing.

In a private, deliberate act of profound faith I lifted my face toward the slanting rays of the late afternoon sun and spoke softly: "Oh my Master, my Friend, my Father, I take of Your very life and drink it to the depths!"

In that moment I sensed the surge of His gracious Spirit flowing into mine to renew and revitalize my ravaged soul. The dynamic of divine life was restoring me.

The second compelling awareness that swept over me was the persistent power and vitality inherent in the flowing waters. They poured over the rocks in gushing torrents that tumbled the small stones along the stream bed. The flowing action wore away rock, shaped stones and carved ever deeper in the hills the channel to the sea.

So it is with the great good will of God. It is an irresistible force in the universe that flows steadily to shape the destinies of us all. His intentions toward us are grand and good and noble. It is His great, persistent power that shapes our history and directs our days.

"The events He allows to intrude upon our little lives are not intended for our undoing," I murmured to myself in quiet soliloquy. "Rather they are intended to conform us to the greatness of His own wondrous character."

The sorrow, the suffering, the shaping of our lives would in time see the contours of our characters likened to His own lofty ideals and purposes for us as His people. Through the deep-cut valleys of our days His own sublime life could flow in refreshment to others who suffered as we did, who tramped the trail of tears that we had trod.

Almost immediately I became acutely aware that out of my own deep grief God could bring balm to other broken lives. He could flow through the anguish and agony of my loss to touch others in their loss.

As the sun warmed my body, caressed my face and sparkled in the stream, I was struck with the remarkable potency of the river. Everything it touched it transformed. There was vigor and vitality in every tree, shrub, blade of grass or mountain flower that flourished on its banks.

It was as if in loud, clear tones it stated boldly, *"Life-life-life!"* Here was the source, the strength, the surge of life itself poured out, spilling over, quickening everything it touched. From this singing, spilling, shining stream came the vitality of all the vegetation of the valley. More than even that, beyond the forest, grass and flowers, were the birds that dropped down here to drink; the wildlife that came here to slake their thirst; the solitary person who came to find new life to face the future.

"O Lord, my God, how generous You are; how gracious to this weary one; how merciful to a man deep in distress!" The words were not spoken aloud. They were the profound inner expression of a spirit being renewed by the gracious inflowing presence of the Living Christ.

He had come to me in the solitude of that high mountain stream and renewed my spirit. Vigor, vitality of divine origin swept into my soul bringing life, life—life from above—from the edge of the sky, from Himself.

It is not surprising that the grand old apostle John in his sublime vision of the eternal city of our God should see a shining stream flowing as a river of life from beneath the very mercy seat and eternal throne of God. There could be no more pure or poetic language in all the earth to describe the glory of the life of God flowing forever to His people.

What he had seen, I, too, in living reality had experienced on this still summer afternoon high in the mountains. New life, dynamic energy and fresh vigor filled my soul from the eternal source of God Himself.

As the evening sun settled slowly over the last high ridges of the sky edge, the warm rays laid a golden glow of sheer glory over the stream. Never in all my years in the wilderness had I seen flowing water take on such wondrous beauty. Breath-taking shades of green and gold, of blue and silver, flashed in the current and gleamed from the running waters.

It seemed almost every color of the spectrum shone like light glinting from a thousand gems that sparkled in the stream. Even the intense whiteness of the tumbling rivulets turned the whole scene into a dazzling display of artistic loveliness.

And again the vivid, moving, majestic realization came to me with shining clarity: *"Life does go on. Life can be beautiful. Life is touched with wonder . . . because of my Father's perpetual presence!"*

My part was to look for the glory of the Lord as it was reflected to my watching gaze from day to day. Just as the sun touched the stream and turned it into a glowing scene of dazzling beauty, so the effulgence of the glory of God could transform my little life into a thing of shining beauty and gentle wonder.

In the evening shadows I strolled back quietly to my camp. The Eternal One had touched my spirit with His Own that afternoon. Healing and help and hope had come flowing to my soul that assured me, *"All was well!"*

7

The Olalla Bush

Long, long before the white settlers pushed their way across the prairies and into the western mountain region, wild serviceberries comprised an important part of the Indian's diet. The prolific purple fruit, similar in size and shape to the better known blueberries, was gathered in great quantities by the various tribes. Some of the berries were eaten fresh, but the greater portion, mixed with animal fat, were made into pemmican. Pemmican was the staple food used on the trail and consumed in severe winter weather.

Out on the prairies serviceberries generally grow as rather stunted shrubs clinging tenaciously to deep draws or cut banks in the coulees. There the hardy bushes find shelter from the blinding blizzards and cutting winds of the long harsh winter.

In our high mountain region with long valleys and sun-splashed slopes facing south, the serviceberry grows into a large imposing clump of sturdy brush. Some of these, in choice locations, will reach a height of fifteen feet, with an elegant vase shape that is almost as wide as it is tall. The long slender limbs are tough, durable wood that can endure the relentless lashing of the wind without ever breaking under its force.

Only when the bush has become very aged and dies from natural causes, do the branches become gray and brittle. Then they will snap under the weight of heavy snow or give way if battered by a bull or shredded by a buck in rut.

The Indian name for our mountain serviceberry is the *Olalla*. It is a lovely name. Its lilting sound is suited to a shrub so beloved by both outdoorsmen and the wildlife of the hills. All winter the picturesque lacelike limbs, shorn of their little round leaves, stand in sharp silhouette on the white slopes where the snow lies deep. They decorate steep rock slides, deep rugged draws and unlikely barren spots where bears, coyotes or wild birds may have dropped the seeds in their dung.

No man, at least to my knowledge, has ever planted an Olalla bush for decoration. Yet in the spring of the year, which comes early in our sheltered upland valleys, the Olallas burst into clouds of delicate beauty. Fragrant clusters of creamy white blossoms decorate the slender branches, hanging in splendid profusion from every twig, like piles of puffed rice.

Their sweet nectar attracts swarms of bees and lesser insects to hover over the blossoms. A gentle, intense hum of wings fills the spring air as each bush welcomes the host of winged visitors. And all across the countryside the billowing white clumps of Olallas embellish the stark slopes and gray rock slides.

Soon the white petals fall in sparkling showers. The breezes blow them in snowy drifts across the ground. In their place come the first fruit and tender green leaves which are browsed eagerly by both game and livestock.

Rapidly the fruit forms. With astonishing speed the

berries swell on the stem. If spring showers are frequent the limber branches soon begin to bend in graceful arcs beneath their heavy load of rich purple berries. In favorable spots the fruit is large and luscious, a banquet for birds, bears, coyotes, chipmunks and passing people.

Indian summer weather finally turns the Olalla leaves to burnished bronze. The edges, trimmed with brown, give the shrub the strange glow of a bush on fire when touched by the sun . . . yet not consumed by the incandescent glory of its own inner light.

One warm day this past summer I went in search of a special bush that I had marked carefully on one of my hikes. It stood all alone on a steep, stony slope far removed from any other bushes of its kind. It was laden with beautiful berries of unusual size. So when they were fully ripe I was determined to return and harvest the wild bounty.

The impressive size of this particular bush was enough to attract my attention. Only because it grew on such a steep slope was it possible to reach the bent limbs that hung down close to the ground on the upper side. There, in the thin shade of its rather sparse foliage, I could readily strip the abundant fruit from the arched branches. In no time at all, my large bucket was filled, heaped up and overflowing with the luscious fruit. Every berry was fully ripe, turgid with juice, sweet to the taste.

Before I had come that morning the wild ones had been there before me. The lower limbs, easily reached by cunning coyotes, had been stripped. The upper clusters had been picked over by the birds. So I was fortunate to find an ample abundance still remained for me to harvest.

As I picked my share I marveled at such bounty coming from an uncultivated, untended tree in such an unlikely spot. Here the soil was thin, stony, riddled with rocks, and baked by the relentless sun. The seasonal winds whipped the bush back and forth without mercy, lashing its limbs with every savage blow. And the heavy loads of winter snows fell upon the branches, bending some to the ground, drifting over its base with ice and frost.

In spite of all the adversities of its environment, all the abuse of rough weather, all the stresses of its stern and tough location, the Olalla bush flowered and fruited in this spot with joyous abandon.

It was a vivid, living demonstration of that ancient adage—"*Just bloom where you are planted!*" It sounds so simple. Sometimes it has an almost romantic touch to it. Like so many spiritual concepts it is often spoken too swiftly and glibly by someone who has never faced the fierce, formidable challenges of living a truly productive life in a most desolate and desperate environment.

Often as I have been out on the mountains, hiking hard on a remote ridge at the edge of the sky, it has startled me to come across a lone Olalla bush, bursting with blossoms or laden with delicious fruit. By the superb miracle of my Father's loving arrangement, beauty of bloom and a banquet of fruit have been distilled from the tough raw materials of stony soil, burning sunlight and hidden underground seeps of moisture.

On the gaunt granite He has laid out some of the most beautiful bouquets in all the earth. And there too He has turned rain, sunshine and gravel into the most delectable fruit and juice for the gentle refreshment of all who pass by.

Our modern preachers and hyper-evangelists urge us to demand our "miracles" from God. They rant at us to claim our rights and receive some sort of dramatic demonstration from the divine. They insist that only by special signs and wonders will the world ever come to acknowledge Christ as God very God.

He Himself told us no such spectacular displays were necessary to demonstrate His deity!

74

 Instead He urged us to look around and quietly notice the lily of the field, the fledgling sparrow fallen from its nest, the Olalla bush blowing in the breeze. There in the ordinary events of the natural world around us lay a thousand miracles of His making, the lovely touch of our Father's care.

It is not that He chooses to deprive us of staggering, mind-bending demonstrations of His splendor. Rather, the difficulty is that we are so slow of spiritual perception, so dull of divine insight that we are impervious to the remarkable display of His magnificent prowess all around us. Eyes we have that do not see and ears that do not hear.

An avalanche lily, pure as the finest gold, pushes its lovely bloom through the snow on some remote mountain meadow. We simply nod our heads in momentary surprise, then stroll on—never considering that no man's hand had any part in such a spectacle, such a complex creation. A skein of geese, hurtling across the loftiest ranges at a steady 60 MPH, hour after hour, dead on course, without the aid of computers or other electronic gadgetry, will find their winter haven 4,000 miles to the south. A gorgeous Olalla bush all aglow in glorious attire, no matter the season— graceful lacework in winter, perfumed blooms in spring, purple with fruit in summer, ablaze with gold in fall—to us dull mortals is all just "part of the scene."

O, to have the scales of human skepticism stripped from our eyes now dimmed by the madness of our man-made media! O, to have the sensitivity of our spirits reborn after being so long imprisoned by the crude and crass culture of our cities! O, to have the strings of our souls stirred once more by the splendor and the glory of our God and Father which in fact fill all the earth!

It takes time, much time, precious time alone, in company with Christ, for the dynamic reality of His life and

light and love to break through the darkness of our delusion and set us free. We do not need to seek some special
services or attend some sensational staged event to witness
the miracles of His power.

The glory of His grace, the loveliness of His presence
can be seen even in the lowly beauty of an Olalla bush. He
surrounds me with new miracles every morning.

It is such an acute awareness of Christ's presence in
the world of plants and trees, grass and flowers, sun and
rain, clouds and earth, moon and stars, sunrise and sunset
that can enable the most ordinary person "to blossom
where you are planted."

One of my dear friends is an elderly widow who lives
in an austere retirement center in the very heart of the
city. Endless traffic and crowds of pedestrians press in
around her residence in a constant cacophony of noise and
confusion. The halls she walks are dim, dark, haunted by
aged people who for the most part have given up hope.
Her own tiny room is almost like a narrow cell with a
limited outlook between the building's concrete walls.

Yet in such a stark setting this loving lady pours out
the perfume of her gracious personality upon every life
she touches. Every day she is fit enough to get out, she
takes walks to pick any stray flowers, or leaves, or even
decorative wayside weeds she can find. These she brings
back to share with others who are shut-in, or in the hospital.

Every book, every pamphlet, every magazine that
comes into her possession she passes on to someone else to
enjoy. Her tiny figure is filled with laughter, fun and the
joyous optimism of one who loves her Father and revels in
His company. The sunshine of the sky, the wonder of the
stars, the fragrance of flowers, the healing touch of trees
and grass are reflected in gentle love from the soul and
spirit of this saint.

Wherever she goes, she leaves behind a legacy of

hope, of cheer, of good will to those she meets. Through her little life there radiates to all around her the character of Christ, the gentle glory of God. She, too, is a living miracle, a divine demonstration of our Father's life touching and transforming her life at the edge of the sky.

For she, too, is like the Olalla bush that blossoms where God has planted her, even among the indigent and dying all around her.

8

Trees above
Timber Line

One of the rare and special thrills of hiking in high country is to break out above timber line into the stillness and solitude of the alp-lands. These lofty alpine meadows lie at the sky edge, wedged between the trees at lower levels and the soaring ice slopes sharp against the sky.

As a younger man I spent weeks and months in these "gardens of God." It was here, where ramparts of rock, ice and snow stood in majesty above the wildflower fields that I stalked the monarch of the mountains, the Grizzly, and the Mountain Caribou, the Bighorn Sheep and hardy Mountain Goats. I was studying their life habits, recording their migration routes, filming the intimacy of their day-to-day behavior.

Amid such grandeur I was always stirred by the solitary trees that found footing and flourished in this harsh and rugged upland realm. Occasionally the trees grew utterly alone, clinging tenaciously to some crack in a cliff or standing sturdily on a rock outcrop where wind and weather lashed them mercilessly. More often they grew in little clusters, a few unyielding individuals giving mutual support to each other in the exposed and perilous paths of hail, sleet, snow and roaring winds.

Unlike animals, birds or men, trees simply cannot shift or move about to protect themselves from the adverse vagaries of weather. Rooted to one spot they must stand there and survive the onslaught of sun, wind, snow, storms, blizzards and all the ravages of time and tempest. The passing seasons and pressure of environmental forces so move upon the tree that often it barely survives the stresses and strains of its formidable setting.

Such solitary trees, wind-twisted and storm-tossed, are not always the perfectly shaped specimens of their kind.

To the onlooker they may appear contorted, misshapen, yes, sometimes even broken and blasted by ice and hail and winter gales. Yet they own a special glory born of adversity. They reflect a unique strength that has stood the stress of a thousand mountain storms. They possess a beauty that can emerge only out of great agony and solitary suffering.

It is this steadfast character of the tough trees above timber line that has elicited my own personal awe, respect and interest. It is this unique quality of grandeur that fascinates the photographer; that excites the artist; that arrests the passerby.

Standing alone at the sky edge, the sturdy trunks, dwarfed and shortened by so much snow and ice, often appear compressed by the constriction of such an arctic climate. The branches, beaten and battered by nonrelenting wind with sleet in its teeth and snow on its wings, seem stubby and foreshortened. Here, one may have been torn away in a roaring gust. There, another may have been bent and twisted like a knotted arm held up in bold defiance against the storms of life. Sometimes the crown has been broken in a winter avalanche of snow and a new leader has emerged to push its twisted trunk into the clouds and mist that swirl through the peaks.

Still the trees survive. Still their sparse foliage reflects the upland sun. Still they stand silhouetted in royal splendor against their gaunt backdrop of snow fields, rock ridges and shining skies at the edge of the horizon. Still they put on new wood from season to season.

In their quiet fortitude lies a stirring example of the benefits of adversity. In their unusual beauty, mortal man can discover something of our Father's grand design for shaping special people.

First of all, it is of more than passing interest that these trees of unusual inspiration are not a part of the full forest of the lower slopes. They are rugged individuals set apart from the common crowd that make up the usual stand of timber. Isolated from their fellows, they are often rooted in some remote spot where they must stand alone against the storms. They do not enjoy the shelter of ten thousand other trees that might offer respite from the wind or shade from the sun.

Their life is spent in the solitude of the sky edge.

Their seasons are passed in the rare upland realm of the alp-lands.

Their life must be lived in the maelstrom of stress at the extreme edge of survival.

And in the economy of God, the same is true of those who are willing to live separated lives, apart from the common crowd of our human society. There is such a thing as being too sheltered by our "comfortable culture"—too coddled by our contemporaries, too indulged by our affluent age.

If certain of us are going to be shaped into special specimens of rare quality, it calls for some suffering alone. Rugged strength is not developed in the soft security of our associates. There has to be that deep grounding of our lives in the very bedrock of Christ's character if we are to endure the blasts of adversity.

Christian leaders speak too easily, too glibly, too romantically of "getting onto higher ground with God." It is almost as if they are inviting their listeners to take a stroll into a summer rose garden.

To get onto a higher life with the Risen Christ demands great discipline from the disciple. It calls for separation from the world's soft and cozy associations. It means strong self-denial, standing alone in noble, lofty living. It entails suffering, sorrow, pain and the drastic endurance of adversity.

Christ came to us as "a man of sorrows and acquainted with grief." He was one cut off from the comfortable, easy companionship of His contemporaries. He stood alone in His suffering that He might prove to us the unfailing fortitude of the living God. Despite the worst the world could hurl at Him, He emerged triumphant—beaten, broken, bruised on our behalf, yet able to bring us to Himself in great glory.

If we of the late twentieth century are to claim His name, then it is incumbent on us to be prepared to be His separate people. The indulgent, soft, cozy church of our day does not challenge Christians to come out from the corrupt culture of our times. It does not demand that we stand boldly, bravely against the blasts of adversity which are bound to assail us. It prefers to keep us soft, sheltered, comfortable and complacent in our padded pews. There we can have our good fellowship, good fun and good food without ever facing the fury of the fierce elements in the world.

Those prepared to be apart, strained and stressed by the agonies of our age, are few and far between. Those who will endure hardship in solitude are rare indeed. Those who, despite the suffering, will stand strong are as thrilling to encounter as any wind-shaped tree at the sky edge.

One dear couple, longtime friends of mine, are of this caliber. Both in their late eighties, bent and beaten by the storms of life, they live in noble dignity. She is blind. He is crippled with arthritis, both hip joints replaced with artificial sockets. Yet every week at tremendous personal pain they visit the aged. She plays the piano while he sings lustily to lift the spirits of those downcast. Season after season, sun or snow, they visit in children's camps to bring inspiration to the young.

This is what it means to live on the high ground of God's choosing apart from the crowd.

This is what it means to see the beauty of the Most High expressed in the humble conduct of His followers.

This is to encounter something of the very character of Christ in a common woman and man of rare loveliness.

Thus amid all the lashing storms of life and winds of adverse suffering there is demonstrated the noble faithfulness of our Father who empowers them to prevail. We look on in awe and wonder, moved and inspired by their brave fortitude, their quiet faith in Christ, their flowing love that uplifts a hundred other hearts.

Turning back to the trees above timber line we see a second dimension to their growth not often recognized by the casual passerby.

It is the rare and elegant quality of the actual wood produced within the wind-tossed trees. Its grain is of exquisite texture interspersed with whorls and curving lines of unusual gracefulness. The stresses and strains of being tossed and twisted by the wind and sleet and deep snows of winter produce an extra flow of resins in the tree. Not only does this give the fibers a remarkable tight-grained texture but it gives off also an exquisite fragrance.

An expert violin maker, who is a master craftsman, tells me that he spends weeks each summer searching for special trees above timber line. From these he takes his choicest material to create musical instruments of the finest quality and tone.

Wood produced in the high and tough terrain above the usual timber stands bears within it a rare timbre and lovely resonance not found in ordinary lumber cut at lower elevations. The fury of storms, the shortness of the growing season, the wrenching of the winds, the strain of survival in such an austere setting—all these combine to produce some of the toughest, choicest, most wondrous wood in all the world.

Here is wood grown on a gaunt rock ridge on some remote mountain range that one day will grace a violin, cello or guitar in Lincoln Center. From those tree fibers will come the finest music ever made by man. Its melodies and notes will enrich a thousand listeners, and, by modern communication, encircle the globe to inspire a million more.

But it all began with a sturdy tree, set apart, growing slowly, unknown, all alone on a distant hill against the sky edge.

Precisely the same principle is true for us as God's chosen people. Choice characters, fragrant lives, rare quality of life are not produced without the strain of sorrow and the suffering of adversity. Some of us will have to endure privation in personal isolation and more than likely without any public acclaim. Most of our inner anguish of soul is borne alone in the solitude of our own lives. We are not public performers, playing to a rapt but fickle audience.

Our greatest griefs are more often than not those of the spirit. Our stresses come most painfully within the very fibers of our souls. The agonizing separation within that attends the onslaught of suffering, the agony of losing loved ones, the betrayal of friends can be healed only by the gracious ministrations of God's own Gracious Spirit.

But He does bind us up. He does inject His own presence into our lives. He does enable us to grow more beautiful, more gracious, more resonant with His compassion.

The end result is that our own characters do become more desirable. We do mature into men and women of wondrous warmth. We do, little by little, develop into fit material for the Master's use.

And out of it all, one day, there will emerge celestial music and glorious melodies that can enrich and uplift others clear around the earth because we grew at the sky edge.

9

Fire on the Mountains

Virtually every mountain in our region has, at some time or other, been scorched by fire. Ridge after ridge bears the ancient scars, now healed over, of drastic lightning strikes. Here and there, because of intense mineralization in the rock formation, numerous old twisted trees are splintered and shattered on the sky edge where the high voltage electrical charges went to ground.

During the severe heat of our long summer weather it is common for gigantic cumulus clouds to build up over the ranges. Out of these huge "thunderheads," with their intense electrical energy, lightning flashes across the uplands and thunder rolls in the deep valleys. It is a moving and majestic display of formidable power in the high country.

Sometimes the electrical display will last for several hours. Blinding light of blue-white intensity illuminates every tree, shrub, rock and peak in vivid clarity. It is a celestial display a thousand times more majestic than any manmade carnival creation with its gaudy lights.

As the thunder rumbles across the high ridges it

resembles the approach of the apocalypse. The tremendous sounds reverberate across the mountains, echo from the canyon walls and boom against the rocks like gunfire in giant battle. When thunder is close by, the earth trembles in the tumult and trees toss about in the tempest of the gusting winds that accompany the electrical storms.

Lightning bolts crash to earth. Fingers of fire like a cougar's long claws reach for the ridges and zigzag across the sky edge. Rocks are shattered. Trees are split and splintered. Dry brush, grass and forest duff explode in flames.

It is all an ancient part of the natural weather forces that have shaped our lofty upland world. Fire has always been a formidable factor in controlling forest growth, regulating the succession of plant communities in the region and removing excessive stands of undesirable timber growth.

Even the primitive Indian races seemed to understand and grasp the benefit of burning off part of the wilderness every year. This way the region was being given the chance to be cleared of undesirable undergrowth. The raging fires removed and consumed low-quality ground cover like cheat-grass and knap-weed that invaded the upland ranges. The searing heat destroyed ravening insect populations and gave the high country a chance for a whole new generation of pioneer plants to be reborn out of the cinders and ashes that remained.

The emergence of new forage and the growth of fresh grass fertilized by the abundant mineral content of the ashes, the stimulation of new and nutritious shoots and seedlings from the scorched earth, all combine to produce a bountiful wildlife habitat that attracts birds and animals in large numbers. This all made for good hunting and in more recent times for better grazing.

Modern forest and range management is beginning to use "controlled burning" as a means to improve and enhance the natural habitat. But before that concept came into use, forest and brush fires were somehow always considered to be a great evil—probably because they were regarded as a profligate waste of valuable timber or the destruction of worthwhile watersheds where dense forest cover is desirable for percolation purposes.

When I was a very young man, one of my early adventures in the western mountains was to work on a fire crew in the Cascade Mountains of Washington. It was a startling and exciting introduction into the high country. The elements of danger and daring that such work demanded nourished my eager spirit of adventure. I fully believe no person has truly lived who has not, at some time, risked his or her very life in a cause greater than himself or herself.

Everything within my make-up responds energetically to the tough demands of a great challenge. My mind is quickened; my emotions are stirred; my will is set like steel to take the test, to run the risk, to overcome the obstacle.

To be on the fire line in midsummer under a blazing sun with the normal outside temperature around 100 degrees is a testing ordeal. Thirst becomes a terrible torture. One's throat is dry and sore as if seared by a hot iron. Excessive perspiration soaks shirts and trousers, leaving the body limp with lassitude. Tears stream from smoke-filled eyes. Often they are irritated and inflamed from cinders, ash, dust and particles of partially burned debris that float in the hot air.

Feet swell in soot-smudged boots heated from tramping across the scorched earth and blackened, smoking soil. Hair and skin are singed. Face and hands are grimed with streaks of sweat and soot, leaving one looking like a derelict, his stained clothes all askew.

This is a measure of a man's mettle.
Here a man's spirit shows true.

What a test of character and will!
This is where a daring spirit glows bright.
Here there is no place for quitters.

All of this is lived out against a raging inferno of crackling flames that rushes through the trees, sweeps up the slopes in a wall of fire, then explodes in the branches above. Showers of burning twigs, glowing bits of flaming bark and cones fall to the forest floor. Huge clouds of blue and black smoke billow up from the burning debris. The sky darkens. The sun is shaded and a great rushing wind develops from the up-draft of the fire's ferocious heat.

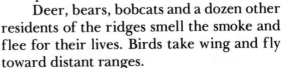

Deer, bears, bobcats and a dozen other residents of the ridges smell the smoke and flee for their lives. Birds take wing and fly toward distant ranges.

All seems to be ruin and desolation.

But things are not always as they appear.

For out of this fire on the mountain, new life will emerge. New growth will come. A fresh forest will be re-created.

Perhaps the most dramatic demonstration of this process in modern times is the renewal of life on the devastated slopes of Mount Saint Helens. Biologists and environmentalists have been startled and delighted to see the incredible resurgence of new life in areas utterly devastated and burned over by the volcanic eruption.

Our lofty western mountains have been born and shaped by fire. Their very character and contours are the end product of burning. Their grand silhouettes against the sky, their mantles of forest cover, grassy ranges and glorious alp-lands all have been shaped by fire. Even the shining "silver forests" of stark fire-scorched trees with their blazing carpets of native wildflowers came to beauty by their burning.

I have mused much over this phenomenon in the natural realm. There is much to meditate over as one sits quietly beside a little campfire in the evening. The gentle crackle of the flames; the inviting warmth of the burning wood; the sweet fragrance of the blue smoke; the pungency of pine sap and spruce gum filling the night air—all promote long thoughts and deep reflection.

There is something profoundly primitive about man and fire. His most ancient traditions and oldest roots are shaped by fire. All the struggles to survive, the preparation of food, the shelter against the bitter wind and biting cold are bound up with fire. Beyond all this the celebration of life, the joy of comradeship, the intimacy of family ties, the offering of sacrifices and incense were entwined with fire—and still are.

Is it any wonder our Lord God sometimes refers to Himself as fire? Are we startled to see so many references in His Own divine revelation to us, as His earth children, that He comes to us as fire? Is it not understandable that even of old He would choose to appear to His chosen ones in flames of fire?

It was a flame of fire that moved among the pieces of Abraham's ancient sacrifice. It was fire and smoke and a great burning that descended in power on Mount Sinai when God's presence came down upon the sacred mountain. It was a divine flame that fell upon Mount Carmel to consume Elijah's bullock as well as even the water and stones of the altar. It was prophesied by John the Baptist that when Christ came He would bring fire on the earth. And visible, tangible evidence of the truth was clearly seen when flames of fire appeared upon the disciples on the Day of Pentecost in the upper room.

In the divine economy of the Most High, fire is an inescapable part of the impact of His presence on us.

That is a comparatively simple statement to make on paper. The reader may pass over it rather lightly. But its true spiritual implications, for the person prepared to take God seriously, are enormously profound.

Most of us do not take the bold, somewhat blunt statements of Scripture very seriously when they speak of fire in the life of the Christian. Too often these comments are relegated to romantic imagery or regarded as rather primitive language for conveying the idea of light, warmth or comfort to man.

We really do not want to deal with the dire results that a genuine conflagration of celestial burning might have on our cozy culture. The modern church of the late twentieth century in North America knows virtually nothing about fire on the mountain. Our fire suppression equipment has become so sophisticated, so ready on standby, so swift to respond to the first spark that smolders, that the Glorious Spirit of the Living Christ can hardly get a good blaze started in any soul!

The fierce burning that comes with shattering conviction of sin is scarcely known today. The sweeping, searing flames of fear of divine judgment and inescapable justice from a righteous God are no longer in the land. The intense inner fires of purification and cleansing and change that once swept through the souls of men like Wesley, Whitfield and Wilberforce are well-nigh a bed of ashes in the comfortable company of the contemporary church.

Where are the men and women today who do actually offer up their lives as a living sacrifice to be consumed in the flames of expendable service to the Most High? Where do we find those willing to be purged and purified by the in-rushing, invading, burning presence of God's Holy Spirit? Where do we see people so cleansed by the incandescent life and light and love of Christ that the corrupt culture of our times does not taint their souls nor stain their spirits?

The in-coming of Christ's presence in power and

great glory is a burning, scorching, searing experience that utterly changes the contours of our characters. Once we have been exposed to the fire of God's own purifying presence the old debris and detrius are destroyed, wiped out, purged from our lives. We are never, ever, the same again.

Only the burning, explosive, raging fires of God the Holy Ghost are ever going to clear the cheat-grass, the knap-weed, the thistles and thorns out of our tangled lives. The time has come when the fierce up-drafts of the wind of His Spirit need to sweep through our comfortable churches and compel people to fall on their faces in humble contrition. The day is long overdue when the fire from above flashes across the skies of our times to come crashing with lightning bolts into the stony ground of our rock-hard hearts. The hour is here when as a rotten society of overindulgent people we again hear the roar and rumble of the majestic voice of our Father calling us to be a cleansed and, respectfully, separate church.

Often as I hike alone in these high hills I cry out to the Most High to descend upon us in great power. I beseech Him to "break out" upon us with a fierce burning. I implore Him to release His Sovereign Spirit to sweep freely and fiercely across the earth convincing men of sin, righteousness and judgment to come.

Unless this happens there can be no renewal.

Only the purifying presence of the Lord God Himself will ever deliver us from our decadence. He alone can bring us new life, new vitality, new beauty.

There has to be fire on the mountains again.

10

Stillness

For some of us the great glory of the high ridges and alpine basins is the sense of utter stillness and quiet grandeur that pervades the sky edge. The mountains were a realm rather far removed from the encroaching noise and clamor of human commerce and industry.

To a degree this is still true. Yet the formidable truth is that even the mountain stillness is being shattered by the increasing invasion of humanity and its mobile equipment. The scream of chain saws, the roar of bulldozers, the thunder of helicopters, the chatter of all-terrain vehicles, the blast of snowmobiles all combine to devastate the pristine stillness of the high country.

One has to go farther and farther afield to find secluded valleys or virgin ranges not yet ravished by the ruthless, grasping hands of modern "civilization." Logging roads and fire trails, recreational developments, mining operations and high-power transmission lines have spun a web of human technology across the wilderness. So it becomes ever more difficult to find a spot where stillness, quietness and true wilderness tranquillity prevail.

But here and there such precious places do remain. The area immediately adjacent to my present home is one of them. Just down the country road that winds through our upland valley is one of the largest radio telescopes in the west. It was located in that lovely mountain basin because of its seclusion. No aircraft are allowed to fly over the area. No chain saws, snowmobiles, dirt bikes or all-terrain vehicles are permitted. No commercial development is to be countenanced.

Here unusual peace prevails. And most of the time a serene stillness enfolds the valley.

As more and more people crowd the planet, it is inevitable that they must adjust to the ever-increasing noise of their civilization. This is especially true of larger metropolitan areas and industrialized urban centers. In those places noise is a way of life. It is a major part of the pressure which makes existence for millions stressful and painful—even though they may not be aware of this tension in their man-made environment.

In such a setting, try as he or she may, it is most difficult for any individual to think long thoughts—to meditate quietly over eternal verities, or even consider carefully the ultimate destiny of day-to-day decisions.

This explains why all through human history, if men were to be set aside for special service to their people, it was demanded that they first find some solitude and stillness where they could commune with their Creator. The ancient patriarchs, the flaming prophets of former times, the seers with burning eyes and great visions, the chosen saints with their profound spiritual perception were invariably those who had found the stillness of the high places, there to listen quietly to the soft solicitations of God's Gracious Spirit.

It is noteworthy that even Christ Himself, when He was here among us, continually separated Himself from the clamor of the crowds. He simply had to detach Himself from the pressure of people and the crush of the cities to find solitude on the mountain slopes. Nor is it mere accident that we are told this again and again by those who were closest to Him.

Finding stillness was an essential part of His life.

He did not neglect this exercise.

It was something He did continually at personal cost and the risk of gross misunderstanding.

It was the sure guarantee that His character would not be compressed or deformed by His contemporaries.

It was in the stillness of the night that He gave Himself to prayer, to meditation and to quiet spiritual communion with His Father. These were interludes of inspiration, uplift and restoration for His spirit.

If such moments were precious to Him, how much more so it must be true for us! It is in these quiet times that we can be open and receptive to the still, small voice of the Most High.

Of course we must recognize that not everyone has the opportunity to slip away into some secluded spot. Some are literally imprisoned in the canyons of concrete and steel that comprise our great cities. Millions more are cramped like cliff-dwellers in their high-rise apartments of brick and glass. So they have little choice but to find a private little nook someplace wherein a particle of privacy may be experienced for a few fleeting moments.

They have my utmost compassion. And, were I restricted as they are, it is quite certain my free spirit would soon be fractured. Within a few weeks my life would waste away in anguish.

For some of us, stillness, solitude and the vast immensity of great open spaces are the very breath of life itself. It is there, and only there, that we seem to discover the well-springs of our spiritual well-being; the source of our

strength in God our Father; the consolation of Christ to heal our deepest wounds; the comradeship of His Spirit to accompany us through the dark valleys of life.

This was utterly true for me when Harvie went on ahead into the realm of repose prepared for him. I needed desperately to rediscover the deep roots of my being in God. I needed stillness in company with Christ to restore my soul. I needed the strong solace of God's Spirit in the place of quietness.

As Harvie's physical strength diminished and the awareness of his imminent departure became ever more acute, I was in need of special grace to face this tearing wound in the fabric of life. There had to be divine reassurance that "all was well" when really from a purely human perspective a great gash of grief was gouging its way through my soul.

He had been such a noble man, so kind in attitude, so full of fun, so delightful to be with. It was unlikely anyone would be soon found to take his place in my affections as a friend.

In agony of spirit I sought for solace at the sky edge. Again and again my feet were turned to the high-country trails that lead away from the scenes of so much sorrow. I simply had to be alone—alone with my inner thoughts, alone with the utter loneliness of my spirit. Alone, yet not alone—for in the stillness of a lofty valley I sensed and knew the presence of my God.

There in the bright, brittle heat of early afternoon I took shelter in the shade of some high altitude trees growing beside a tiny mountain stream. Not unlike Elijah of old I cast myself down in their cool shadows in anguish of soul. It was not out of self-pity but out of a sense of profound pain at the apparent pointlessness of life. It was all so fleeting, so transient, so fragmented. Nothing appeared to endure, to last, to stand the passage of time.

What were the excruciating events of life doing to the

contours of my character? This was not the first time I had passed through the searing flames of grievous losses in the circle of my family and friends. Again and again grief, separation and deep personal pain had swept through my life. What was the profound purpose in it all?

As I lay inert in the shade of the wind-stunted trees a gentle breeze began to blow through their boughs. It was cool, fresh, clean, coming from the snow-sheathed peaks that glistened white and blue above me. At first the movement of air was so light, so delicate, so nebulous, it seemed only an illusion. Its very essence only seemed to intensify the stillness of the hour.

But that mountain breeze bore on its gentle breath a message more moving than any I ever heard in any man-made sanctuary of steel and concrete. It spoke to my spirit in tones as clear and concise as any borne to me by the thrilling notes of a great organ:

> *"All the earth is in constant change.*
> *Even these majestic mountains weather away.*
> *The granite rocks are worn down by water.*
> *The giant valleys grow ever deeper.*
> *No tree, no shrub, no flower endures.*
> *The clouds come and go. So, too, night and day.*
> *The birds take wing. The insects perish.*
> *Even the bear, the buck and the chattering chipmunk*
> *are here but a breath in time.*
> *All is change. All is passing. All is perishable.*
> *Be still and know that I am God.*
> *Only I endure. Only I remain. Only I change not!"*

In utter silence of spirit I lay prostrate. In total quietness of soul I remained silent. In complete surrender of body I did not move a muscle.

I, a mere man, was alone with my Maker.
It was from Him that I had come.
It was to Him that I would return.
He and He alone was from everlasting to everlasting.

106

Only in Him was there life eternal that could surmount all the exigencies of my little life. Like the breeze from the snowfields, His very life enfolded me on every side. From the day of my creation He had breathed into my being the very breath of His own eternal Spirit. All my life He had sustained and supported me by that same still Spirit that surrounded me on every hand and pursued me along every trail I took. Now in the face of death He, the Gracious Spirit of the Eternal God, in wonder and awe opened my tear-dimmed eyes to behold again the glory and hope our Father gives His children as they cross over to the other side.

He and only He could prepare for us a place of peace.
Soon Harvie would be there to repose in quietness.
The struggle and strain to survive would be over.
All would be well.
All was well!

He was here. . . . Peace!

The cooling breeze picked up strength as the quiet hours passed. It moved through the trees as surely as the breath of a master musician drawing lovely notes from his woodwind instrument. There was music in the wind, celestial music of the Master's making. It brought solace, comfort and healing to my aching heart. There was divine therapy in the gentle movement of the air that cooled my fevered face and dried my tear-stained cheeks.

When I first came to this still spot, it seemed I was so much, so very much alone. In the agony of my anguish, like Mary on the resurrection morn, it seemed no one else was there. Through her tear-blinded eyes she saw only dimly the outline of the empty tomb, the grave shapes of the gaunt gray olive trees.

But in that grim garden there was also the Lord of

Glory—her Master—Rabboni. He spoke her name and she knew Him. In ecstasy she fell at His feet. And so, too, did I on this sparse mountainside.

There broke through again into my awareness the acute revelation: "O Christ, You never do leave us; You never do abandon us to the vagaries of life's constant changes; You never do let us tramp the trail of tears alone. You are ever near, ever dear, ever here."

Slowly, but surely, the long hours of that long summer day slipped by. Steadily the sun sank lower and lower in the western skies until it almost touched the horizon at the sky edge. For the first time that day I felt strong enough to rise and freshen my face with the cool water that ran in the tiny stream at my feet.

I bared my legs to the sun and let the mountain breeze run its fingers through my tousled hair. New vigor, fresh vitality, supernatural life began to course through my being. In quietness and in peace my strength was being restored. I was in the hills alone yet not alone, for there my strength was coming from my Father.

Suddenly a beautiful butterfly fluttered down the stream bed. It settled on my sun-warmed leg. There it paused briefly to preen itself and fold its gorgeous wings in quiet contentment. What a flash of glory, a splash of light, a touch of wonder to a wounded spirit!

Then from the rock-ribbed slope above me came the clear call of a Vesper Sparrow singing in a stunted spruce. The sun settled behind the western ranges. Long shadows crept down the valley as darkness began to descend.

But the sparrow's liquid notes filled the darkening twilight. The melodious tones rippled down the hill to me. Truly this was a song in the night! The grief was gone. In the stillness God had touched my sorrow. In the dawn there would be a new song in its stead.

11

The Season's First Heavy Snow

Autumn comes gently into our segment of the western mountains. Very seldom does the warm weather season end abruptly with the advent of raging blizzards or crushing ice storms as happens in some high country.

The progressive pageantry of fall colors and wildlife movements is one of the most magnificent natural spectacles on the continent. It may not be quite as sensational as the sudden flaming of the famous eastern hardwoods. But it is much more majestic because of the magnificent mountain backdrop that surrounds us on every side.

Indian summer can be the most glorious season of the entire year. The golden days splashed across the sleepy upland valleys are in a mellow mood. A soft blue haze hangs in the warm atmosphere. Ridge after ridge rises against the sky edge in serried ranks, each a little more faint—and lighter blue—as it reaches the farthest horizon.

The stunningly clear desert skies are alight with stars at night, sharp with the first frost and alive with the haunting, lilting cries of the coyotes. The same wide skies by day ring with the ancient, thrilling call of Sandhill Cranes crossing the mountains, of Canada Geese in wavering V's moving southward from the icy arctic.

In the mountain draws Vine Maples and Western Sumac flame like fire against the golden bunch grass hills. Along the streams and lakes, groves of Trembling Aspens and beautiful Black Birch are pure gold or burnished bronze. On the rock ridges Western Larch, some two hundred feet tall, wave their brilliant banners against the blue skies.

Little lakes and upland ponds are so still, smooth and shiny at this special time their surfaces shine silver like polished mirrors. Only here and there a flock of ducks or a passing deer, pausing to drink, will disturb the scene.

It is all so serene, so peaceful, so calm one could wish this gentle season would endure much longer than it does. Then one morning there is a glistening mantle of immaculate white draped softly over the highest crest of the loftiest peaks. The sky edge is adorned with the first fresh snow to touch the earth this autumn.

Though so far away, it is a clear, shining signal that the mountains are beginning to cool down. The gradual drop in temperatures is a gentle warning that winter is approaching. And with the advent of the icy season, strong winds, darkening skies and heavy snowstorms will move in from the gray immensity of the Gulf of Alaska.

The advance breezes that blow down the slopes are brisk and chill. They rattle the aspen leaves, stripping them from the white-barked trees. The gusting winds whine in the pines sending down showers of brown needles, old cones, bits of bark and broken twigs. The maples, sumac, birches and larch are shorn of their glowing foliage. Now they stand stark and bare, their dark gray frameworks gaunt against the lowering skies.

Hard frost turns the last green grass a soiled and

saddened brown. Ice begins to creep across the lakes
and ponds locking them in a gray shell. Bit by bit the
whole upland world is transformed into a realm of rock-
hard soil frozen solid. An eerie silence steals across the
valleys. The songs of birds are stilled. All the earth is
waiting for winter.
Then one night it comes!
Snow begins to fall. Ten million times ten million
drifting flakes, each perfect and distinct in pattern, float
down out of the heavy overcast. They drift down through
the trees, settle among the shrubs, adorn every twig, cone,
blade of grass or stone upon the ground.
The storm is not noisy. It does not come in with
roaring force or thundering tones. It is almost imperceptible, yet utterly irresistible. Flake by flake, moment by
moment, hour upon hour, it impresses itself upon the entire landscape.
Nothing escapes its impact. The whole world is suddenly being transformed by the pervasive whiteness. Everywhere the contours of the countryside are softened and
smoothed with the enfolding mantle that crowns every
stone, stump or broken fence rail.
Inch by inch the snow deepens. Two, four, five, perhaps even seven or maybe ten inches will settle out of the
first heavy storm. Glowing pristine pure, it lies unmarked
by a solitary track, untouched by a single hand. For a few
brief moments before break of dawn the land lies immaculate in its dazzling whiteness.
Nothing stirs.
It is a moment of magnificent splendor.
A total transformation has come over the earth.
Exquisite loveliness has erased every scar upon the
land. The last trace of waste, the worst signs of damage
and devastation are covered over by the gracious mantle of
gleaming purity.
As the sun breaks through from behind the scattering

storm clouds a trillion sequins sparkle on the surface of the snow. Uncounted jewels of ice crystals catch the early light and reflect it in brilliant hues like a million diamonds shining in the sun.

Yesterday I went out to walk alone in the silence that follows such a snowfall. I climbed a remote ridge that stood sentinel above a broad upland basin of rolling hills. The whole world was wrapped in white, pensive, pure and still unmarked by man or his machines.

It was a morning to think long thoughts—as far-reaching as the distant views that stretched fifty miles to the far horizons of the sky edge. These were precious moments to muse over the meaning of life. They provided a gentle interlude in which I could be open and receptive to the soft, still impulses of God's Gracious Spirit.

It came home to me with intense clarity, equal to the brightness all about me, that just as the earth needed this great snowfall to make it utterly lovely, so, too, my life needed the enfolding purity of Christ's life to cover all my deficiencies. The ancient prophet of old, Isaiah, spoke of this in eloquent and moving language when he declared on God's behalf:

> *"Come now, and let us reason together,*
> *saith the* LORD: *though your sins be as scarlet,*
> *they shall be as white as snow"* (Isaiah 1:18).

There just have to be times in a person's life when the past is past, when bygones are bygones, when the gaunt, gray, forlorn memories of a former glory are buried under the supernatural loveliness of a new life from above.

For all of us there have to be new beginnings. There have to be fresh moments when we stand on a new height of land and look with widening eyes upon fresh vistas of our Father's great intentions for us. He and He alone can come down upon our soiled souls, our grieving spirits, our wounded hearts to enfold them in His wondrous ways.

As an author it is natural that I should always see life like a book. It is an unfolding tale that is being told chapter by chapter. Though it may appear superficially as one continuous whole, in reality it is not, for each of our lives is fragmented into segments. Each section has a significant beginning and a very specific end. And when that chapter is closed, it is closed! Then comes the time to move on to new adventures, to tackle new challenges, to reach for new insights, to find wider service with the Most High.

Just as summer gives way to fall, then in turn autumn is superseded by winter, so in the life of God's person there are succeeding steps by which we are led to follow Christ and pass from scene to scene in the grand pageantry of His purposes for us.

Summer is not fall. Nor is the autumn winter. Each is a season to itself. Each has a special splendor of its own. But likewise each has the fall-out of wasted opportunities, squandered time, wrong choices and willful waywardness that mar the memories of our better moments.

From time to time these demand a drastic change. There has to be a clean-up of the clutter, a renewal of the soul, a cleansing of the conscience, a fresh effulgence of Christ's life from above and a new falling of God's Spirit upon us to bring beauty into our spirits.

Like the chill winds of November, the stern events of our little lives can quickly make our days seem gaunt with grief and grim with the struggle to sustain enthusiasm. Some seasons it seems sorrow is added to sorrow until only the gray framework remains of what had once been beautiful and bright adventures. In the past eighteen months my wife and I have shared in the deepening gloom of no fewer than fourteen families who faced the scourge of terminal illness.

At such times of stress and distress a man needs more than sentiment or sympathy. He needs more than pious platitudes or easy pleasantries. He needs God—in all His majesty and glory and might!

Only the transforming touch of the Risen Christ upon the life can change the dark contours of the circumstances. He alone can descend upon the darkness of the soul in sorrow, bringing exuberant brightness and whiteness to dispel the doubts and gloom. He alone can transform the very outlook from one of despair to that of eager anticipation.

If this is to happen then we must be open and receptive to the presence and power of the Living Lord who gladly comes to engulf us with the wonder of His own person.

As I stood alone upon that snow-mantled mountain there came to me clearly the awareness that my Father, in His mercy and generosity, could again make all things bright and beautiful in my life. It was He who could erase the resentments at the grievous loss of my friends. It was He who could heal the deep hurt of seeing so much suffering. It was He who could cleanse away the criticism of so much pain and pathos.

Yes, there had been scarlet stains upon my soul. It was not a question of hiding them from Him. Rather it was a time to admit them openly, to lay them honestly before Him, to see that only the profound out-pouring of His Own wondrous life could ever cover them completely with the purity of His presence.

I came down off that snowy ridge a man renewed with a right spirit within me. I had met my Master at the edge of the sky. And in His own winsome way a tremendous fall of fresh snow, His righteousness, was enfolding all my life and outlook.

All would be well! Hope came afresh.

Not only was there hope for today, but even more exciting, hope for the years ahead.

Just as the first great fall of snow spoke of much more than the white splendor of the moment, so the presence of God's Spirit was a promise of new and exciting days to come. Winter was not the end of the seasons, it was but the preparation for spring. So sorrow was not the termination of time but the prelude to a new era of delight ordained for me by a loving, caring Father.

The deep blanket of snow draped across this high country would suckle the springs and replenish the streams that flowed from these slopes next April. The snow pack was the sure guarantee that next summer sparkling lakes would stand filled with cool, clear water to nourish a dry and thirsty land. Because these mountain slopes were buried under snow, ten thousand acres would flourish with emerald-green pastures next year—a carpet of wild-flowers would be flung over the slopes. Herds of wild game would flourish on the bunch-grass ranges.

And so it was I saw clearly again the profound lessons that my Lord was imprinting indelibly upon my crushed and suffering spirit. Out of this pressure of pain, this stress of sorrow, would eventually flow streams of refreshment to others in the days to come.

Only out of the crucible of our calamities can there come the poured-out life that, though crushed, releases the fine wine of selflessness to enliven others amid their anguish. Yes, out of death comes life. Out of despair comes love. Out of darkness comes light.

It is always so with God. He is the source of all hope. And it is He who imparts Himself to me.

12

Puma

"Puma" is the very ancient native name for a Mountain
Lion. In more recent times it has been replaced by such
titles as Cougar or Panther. Of them all, "Puma" is by far
the most appropriate and descriptive. For in its soft sound
there is bound up all the stealth, strength and smooth
conformation of the great cats of the western mountains.

That is the name I bestowed on a small, stray waif of a
kitten that wandered out of the woods near our home one
autumn day. The poor, wee creature was only a few weeks
old, a mere bundle of thin bones and somewhat ragged
skin. Yet even then, she bore the tawny, tabby markings of
a wild cougar and moved with the quiet stealth of a mature
mountain lion.

Of course she was not a true cougar kitten, but a tiny
stray that someone lost by accident while traveling through
our area. Or perhaps she was another kitten dropped off
deliberately by some cruel and uncaring person who as-
sumed she could survive on her own in the bush.

Anyway, it was a special mercy that she allowed my
wife to pick her up and bring her to our little chalet among

the pines. There she found a home where Ursula's tender care, and my own deep affection for all things wild, would assure her of a contented sanctuary.

She immediately surprised us with the unusual warmth of her affection. So many cats are rather aloof and distant in their demeanor. But from the moment we first met, this tiny bundle of life displayed the most moving gratitude for the love and kindness shown her. She immediately crawled up into my lap and began to purr up a storm.

That habit has never changed. If anything, it has intensified. She just loves to be with us, near us, a part of us. When I go to greet her in the morning she immediately responds with a soft mew as if to say, "So nice to see you, boss!" Then she stretches her sturdy body to its limit and reaches up to "touch noses" with me for a morning kiss. All the while she is purring like a well-oiled engine.

Puma came to us at a time of the great sorrow in our life of which I have written earlier in this book. It is inevitable that when friends and beloved associates pass on, there are genuine gaps of great grief left in our lives. This is bound to be true if our friendships are pure and profound. Separation of this sort tears a strip out of the fabric of our affections. And those wounds need more than mere words to heal the hurt and bind up the bruises.

My own conviction is that as humans we need something as strong as the consoling Spirit of God Himself to occupy the void. For those of us who truly know God as our Father, and Christ as our closest Friend, the presence of the Gracious Spirit of the Most High brings new life to our heavy hearts. He gives comfort to our sorrowing spirits. He supplies His Own vital energy to our emotions under deep distress.

In addition to all of which, from time to time, He sees fit to fill the empty place with a new life form as tangible as a bird, a kitten or even perhaps a colt. It is no accident that

ravens were sent to feed Elijah in the terrible wastes of the Trans-Jordan region. It was no mere curiosity that a dove descended to settle upon Jesus at His baptism in the Jordan when He had returned from His awesome temptation in the desert. It was no happenstance that an unbroken colt quietly carried Christ into Jerusalem amid all the mayhem of the fickle crowds who shouted "Hosanna."

Certainly from my own personal perspective, God, my Father, could not have provided us with a more appropriate token of His profound concern than Puma. For into the drabness of our despair she suddenly brought unbounded delight. Amid the grief she brought endless good cheer and incredible gaiety.

Under Ursula's constant generosity and loving care,

the kitten began to fill out in a remarkable manner. In just a few days her coat began to shine like satin. Quite obviously she had some Russian Blue blood in her make-up. For her fur, though unusually short, was thick and dense as the finest plush. It could readily resist the most intense cold of our mountain climate. To the touch it was as soft and smooth as the purest silk.

We have had her now for nearly four months. She has matured into a magnificent creature. She weighs well over ten pounds, a splendid specimen of grace and strength. She had survived in the bush by catching crickets, beetles and butterflies. In those weeks when she struggled to survive on such spartan fare she quickly learned to be swift and sure in her pursuit of any winged prey.

She has not forgotten her early skills. She is death to any fly, spider, wasp or insect that ever dares to enter through our great sliding doors. She can leap three feet in the air and catch an insect on the wing, so swift are her muscles.

Curled up on our laps, she literally revels in being stroked. She lays back her head, closes her eyes in quiet ecstasy, inviting us to tickle her chin or caress her cheeks and ears. She responds with pronounced, powerful purrs that rumble across the room in sheer animal pleasure. In all of this there is enormous contentment, gentle gratitude and profound affection.

We can only guess how old Puma is. At most she is not more than seven months of age. Though big, strong and swift she carries all the traits of a young and playful juvenile. At dusk she races around the house, which is very open in design, with wild abandon. She literally flies over the furniture, fights furiously with phantom foes in the form of tumbling golf balls or soft pom-poms on a string.

Her wild and unpredictable antics at times resemble those of an acrobatic monkey more than a cat. She has a favorite high-backed chair that she climbs over. On it she does acrobatics with incredible dexterity. All of which sends us into paroxysms of laughter. At times her antics are so absurd, so hilarious, so downright delightful I literally roll on the floor in glee.

All such good cheer, good will and glorious therapy could not be purchased at any price. I consider them a beautiful bonus bestowed upon us by the loving provision of our Heavenly Father. He, more than any of our human friends, knew how deeply we needed this element of gaiety, spontaneity and outright physical release in our lives.

Fortunately our furniture, of very simple design, but constructed from the toughest fabrics, has withstood all the onslaughts of Puma's claws with remarkable endurance. Hardly a piece shows the wear and tear of her energetic games. Here and there a claw mark scars the window frames where she climbs to view the wide world that stretches to the sky edge. But that is a small price to pay for so much joy co-mingled with the glorious memories of her happy coming.

Puma is a most astute animal. She seems well able to hold her own amid any company that comes to our home. She never runs or hides or cowers in a corner. Instead, she conducts herself with gentle dignity. She greets each guest with gracious good will.

She will accept discipline without sulking or holding any sort of grudge against the one who administers it. This is a most admirable trait! She is always quick to come back and make up. There are no old hostilities, no unsettled scores, no signs of attempts at revenge. She takes things in stride, is full of forgiveness and eager for good will.

All of this has been a tremendous tonic for me. If only human beings were more like my Puma—less prone to look for hidden motives, less given to holding grudges, less likely to think the worst. What a wonderful place the world might be!

With all of my rough and ready ways she has accepted

me fully just as I am, as her loving friend. Despite my lack of consistency in every detail of life, she finds it fun and adventurous to share my days and enjoy our escapades. For Puma life is a game filled with new challenges. She does not live by the tired old theme of "safety first." And in large measure she has helped to reinject this dynamic dimension of excitement into my own outlook again.

She will pursue any bluejay that taunts her, to the topmost branch of our tallest pines. Tumbling and clawing, she will come scratching her way down without a particle of fear. She will chase her own shadow across the thick cedar shakes of our roof as if it was a game for the gods.

Yes, Puma has come into our lives blown here as it were by the inscrutable wind and wonder of the Great Spirit of our God. She is without a doubt a precious provision for two people in their pain. She has come to us as an angel in disguise. And because she came we are facing the future with great good will tinged by bright new hope.

13

Healing of the Hills

Looking south and west from the great open windows of our home in the hills there stands on the horizon, at the extreme edge of the sky, a dark forested ridge. On clear spring days or under summer skies it is a rich green color with its cloak of pine and fir forests. In the fall it is often a misty blue almost lost to view against the hazy autumn skies. In winter it is the first of our adjacent heights to be rimmed in hoarfrost or mantled in a thick blanket of new snow.

Harvie and I often hiked this range. Somehow, because it was somewhat off the beaten tracks, few people were familiar with this lofty realm. In pioneer days it had been well-known to the hardy prospectors, rugged gold miners and tough old loggers who took all they could from its slopes. Even the earliest skiers, who had used its open slopes facing south and west for their sport, had long since moved to higher mountains with deeper snow. In more recent times it became a summer range for cattle ranchers.

Wherever our tramps across this high terrain took us, there remain grim reminders of days gone by when the tough teams of sturdy horses, and rugged boots of gold seekers, or bush loggers, tore the heart out of these hills.

Such spots had a special fascination for Harvie. He had a passionate love for the mountains, but particularly for those places plundered by man. In part this was because much of his life he had made his own livelihood by hauling tons of ore or logs out of the hills on treacherous winding roads. He seldom spoke of the great nostalgia which seemed to pervade his spirit about these intervals in his life.

On the other hand he expressed great concern over the carnage and waste of resources one saw wherever the ruthless hand of man had been at work. He often spoke vehemently of governmental policies that encouraged exploitation of the environment. His usual calm and cheerful demeanor would become aroused, angry and incensed by the sight of great gashes of cut-over country. His eyes would flash with fire when we passed beautiful mountain meadows or ice-fed streams marred by unbridled and selfish slashing of trees and soil.

Though he had worked hard all his life to wrest a living from the high country, still he held the hills in quiet reverence and loving respect. He knew and sensed with that profound intuition of spirit so seldom found in the sons of frontiersmen, that our very life reposed in a proper care of the earth. He knew that the earth did not belong to us to plunder, rape and abuse. Rather, he understood that we belonged to the earth, whose grandeur could only be preserved and perpetuated by the wise and prudent use of its bountiful resources.

Harvie and I often spoke of these things as we hiked the lofty ranges together. Often we sat beside a stream or high on a windswept ridge and mused over the future of this high, wild realm of rock, ice, open range and vanishing forests. What would it hold for our children and grandchildren? Would the snow-fed streams still run clear in these mountain valleys? Would there be feed left on these winter ranges to support a flourishing population of deer, grouse, mountain sheep and other native wildlife? Would these hills be healed so that in years to come another cutting of timber could be taken from the forest?

In a sentence it might be asked, "Could the destruction and devastation of a generation be renewed and restored in our time?"

I can recall with utter clarity the last time we climbed the faint, high, snow-covered ridge visible from my windows. It was mid-January. Winter had clamped its hard icy grip upon the country. Deep snow had fallen. The whole upland world was a spotless white. We climbed steadily toward the summit. Harvie was keen to show me the old mine shafts that had been sunk into the slopes above timber line.

Step by step, as if in slow motion, we took turns breaking trail through the deep snow. It hung heavy in the dark brooding trees. It clung to our boots, dragged heavy on our pantlegs, slowed our upward progress. Wisps of white vapor drifted about our faces from the heaving of our lungs and exhalation of our breath.

At last we broke out above timber line. And just as we did, the winter sun, too, broke out from behind the low-hanging winter clouds. Suddenly the whole upland realm was wrapped in blinding light and ultra whiteness. One could only see by squinting the eyes to mere slits. The world was wrapped in beautiful brilliance. Then as we reached the sun-swept meadows, pristine whiteness swept away beneath our gaze to the very edge of the sky in every direction. It was as if we were suspended in space where time stood still and not a single sound stirred in the great eternal silence.

It was as if momentarily we stood reverently, almost breathlessly, in the sublime sanctuary of the Most High. Neither of us spoke. It would have been a desecration. An interlude in time, it was a moment in our lives when eternity could be sensed in the soul, known by the spirit. For with intense awareness we were aware: "O God, our Father, You are here! The majesty of Your might and the glory of Your presence fill the earth and sky!"

A few drifting clouds crossed the face of the sun. Quickly we found shelter from the cold against the trunk of a gnarled, old, weather-beaten fir. There we broke out our sandwiches and washed them down with steaming cups of hot tea from the thermos in our packs. The burning liquid flowed through us like molten lava, driving out the frost and chill that penetrated our heavy winter clothes.

Suddenly a dense cloud of heavy fog moved up out of the distant valley below us. In a matter of moments it engulfed us in thick, dense folds of gray vapor. The sun was gone. And a darkness, almost like dusk, enshrouded the hills.

We started down the slope, glad to follow our own deep footprints in the snow. At least we would not need to search for a trail. Tired but deeply contented we tramped homeward, well rewarded for the efforts of the day, weary in muscle and tendon, but exhilarated in mind and emotions.

Harvie had often lamented to me the dreadful devastation of this particular range. Yet on this glorious day it had lain before us cloaked in pristine splendor. So I promised myself I would come there again to see it the following summer. And I did. But Harvie was not with me. He lay at death's door in a hospital over two hundred miles away.

What I saw would have cheered his spirits and lifted his morale. For a great healing had come to the hills. As I climbed the summit a pair of coyotes called across the open grasslands. A Mule Deer doe and her fawn bounded down the slope. A profusion of wildflowers flung themselves beneath the trees and over the ridges. A new forest of young and vigorous saplings covered the old mine scars and rotting stumps. Healing was everywhere!

That morning sparkling droplets of dew hung like suspended sequins of silver from every blade of grass, twig of tree and flower petal. A score of bird songs rose and fell with the symphony of soft mountain breezes that played through the timber. A pair of grouse burst up out of the dense grass before my boots; a big black bear had left his claw marks high on the snow-white bark of a poplar near a spring.

Life, new and fresh and vigorous, was all around me. The very pulse and power of renewal were at work in the upland world. None of it was planned by man nor programmed by science. Rather, it was the regeneration and restoration of a ravaged land by the inherent life and vitality of the biota itself. Once again these hills were becoming beautiful, beautiful! Once again fresh new forests

133

would replace the carnage of cut-over country. Once again wildlife and wildflowers would flourish over a wasteland of old mine heaps and torn-up terrain.

This has always been our Father's way with the earth, so scarred, abused and ravaged by man.

And likewise it is always our Father's way with the soul of man so wounded, torn and scarred by sin, sorrow and the sickness of our society.

Only in Him can there be found the help, the healing, the health that restores us from utter ruin. Few people see this. Even fewer ever understand it. Most men and women do not have eyes to see nor ears to hear what is going on upon the earth. The understanding of their souls is too sotted with sorrow; their spirits are too stained by stress; their hearts are too tough, tempered by hard knocks, to grasp what God in Christ is doing in the world.

Most of us behave as though He did not exist. We act as if He were not here. In fact, in our puny pride we demand He prove Himself by some strange sign or wonder.

But our Father does not function in that way. He does not indulge us with dazzling fanfare. He does not turn to stunning theatrics to impress us with His power.

Instead, He proceeds quietly to restore our souls just as He restores the ravaged hills. He brings His own wondrous healing to our wounded hearts in the same way He heals the flattened forests and binds up the broken ranges. He renews our spirits exactly as He quickens again the streams and springs of the high country—*by the gentle incoming of new life amid the desolation . . . yes, the miracle of His own life at work in the world.*

Everywhere one turns in the high hills of which I speak there is evidence of profound forces at work not arranged by the mind of man. On the gusting winds new seeds are blown in from afar that will revegetate the mountainsides. Birds and small mammals and even bears will distribute the new life germs in their droppings for miles across the country.

New growth will spring up wherever the soil has been disturbed, torn and trampled by the ruthless machinery of modern technology. When the whine of the chain saws, the roar of bulldozers and the thunder of trucks have departed, grass and herbs and brave pioneer plants will steal back softly to cover the scars and bind up the soil again.

I knew and sensed all of this as I stood on the summit of that range later in the summer. All about me on every side there was precious life pulsing strongly in the trees, in the undergrowth, in the riot of wildflowers, in the songs of the birds, in the abundance of big game. What had been a waste was becoming a wonderland.

So it is, too, of any person who will give God a chance to carry out His Own wondrous miracles of grace, mercy, compassion and restoration in the stony soil of their souls. Our greatest difficulty is that far too often we resist His coming into our experience; we close ourselves off from the healing of His presence; we harden our wills against the gracious work of His Gentle Spirit.

In addition to all of that, most of us want an instant fix. We want immediate renewal. We demand an overnight remedy for all our hurts.

We will not give God in Christ either the time or opportunities to bring us back from the bleak disasters that overwhelm us. Instead we turn to every sort of human device or man-made technology in an attempt to find consolation and comfort amid the chaos of our calamities.

The one great lesson I have learned above and beyond all others amid the great distress of recent months is this: *Be still, be quiet, be calm, and know that I am God!* It takes time to do this. It means one must, by a deliberate act of the will, learn to repose confidently in Christ . . . to rest assuredly in the faithfulness of our Father.

He is our hope.
He is our healing.
He is our helper.

The wondrous work which He accomplishes in our souls is done in silence. It is nothing less than the persistent in-coming of His Own Presence to generate within us new life, new vitality, new confidence to carry on. He actually transmits to us His hope, His love, His energy, His ability to begin anew.

As the inspired poet wrote so long ago: "I will lift up mine eyes unto the hills, from whence cometh my help. My help cometh from the Lord, which made heaven and earth" (Psalm 121:1, 2).

As is the healing of the hills, so, also, is the healing of my spirit. Blessed be His name!

14

Wonder Springs Anew

Wonder, awe and enthusiasm comprise a tightly woven, three-strand initiative, which can be one of the most powerful influences to propel us through life. Often this is the element so quickly extinguished when the spirit is submerged, sunk down in sorrow.

> Wonder seems to evaporate.
> Awe slips away silently.
> Enthusiasm wanes like light fading at dusk.

Each of them is uniquely a gift from God. They come to us wrapped up in the irrepressible buoyancy of childhood. And, often, they are most readily restored through contact with a child. The contagion of seeing again through the eyes of a youngster, the wonder of sensing anew the glory of the earth through the senses of a child—these are delightful moments of restoration for one in the twilight of life.

This was the case for me when one of our eight grand-children came to spend several days with us. He is an un-usual lad of gentle disposition and quiet demeanor. His tousled head of hair gleams gold like a ripe field of wheat. His bright, bright blue eyes are clear, limpid and shining like a lake under summer skies. His tanned cheeks, sun-browned arms and lanky legs are smooth like the brown bark on a young birch tree.

We decided to spend a day hiking in the hills to-gether. More than half a century separated us in age, but a steel-like bond of love for all things wild and free bridged the great span of time. We were content in each other's company. With my well-worn binoculars slung over his shoulders, and each of us with a brown bag of sandwiches in hand, we set off for some secret little marshy lakes I knew well.

We had scarcely started up the dusty summer trail when we came to some Olalla bushes hanging heavy with rich dark berries. Though we had eaten a hearty break-fast, the delicious, winelike fruit lured us to stop briefly and relish the richness of its flavor.

Den (his full name is Dennis) had never set his teeth into wild fruit of this sort before. As the sweet juice of the berries burst in his mouth and trickled over his lips and tongue he could scarcely restrain his pleasure. The low, contented grunts of a boy in utter joy rumbled in his throat. His young face split into broad smiles now stained wine purple with the pungency of the fruit. He could eat all he wished. The wild bounty was his. It was free for the taking. He reveled in its abundance.

Somehow Olalla berries had never tasted so sweet to me before. As the blue stains marked our lips and moist-ened our fingers we sensed we were feasting the way wild bears and birds eat. For they too had banqueted on these bushes.

There were the distinct paw marks of a young bear

in the dust on the path. We could see where the bushes were broken and battered by his harvesting. Along the trail the fresh dung of his passing was still soft under the morning dew.

Excitement, wonder and enthusiasm began to build between us. If we walked silently and softly, perhaps we would encounter him over the next knoll. Maybe it would be our pleasure to find the furry fellow feeding in another clump of berries.

As we started to climb the sage-covered slope a whole flock of young magpies burst up out of the tall brown grass. They were catching beetles, grasshoppers and ants. The current year's fledglings, such noisy but handsome birds, flew into some nearby trees and upbraided us for disturbing them.

I had seldom seen so many magpies in a single flock. Their raucous cries, their flashing black and white wings, their erratic flight from branch to branch of the Ponderosa Pines suddenly filled the hills with color, action and life. Both of us stood still, enthralled by all the flashing movement. We grinned from ear to ear.

Gently I led Den to a nearby clump of sturdy, thorny hawthorns. There the rough, ungainly, tangled masses of twigs wedged between the branches were a dead giveaway as to where most of the young magpies had been hatched and reared. The huge unsightly nests were vacant now. But in the future he would know where to look for the cunning birds that are such a menace to their lesser neighbors.

We came over the crest of the hill we were climbing. There below us, nestled like two silver plates shining in the sun, held in the hollow of the hills, were a couple of spring-fed ponds. Not too many people know about them. Only the local ranchers who graze their cattle on this high summer range are familiar with these waters.

Den gasped in startled wonder at the sight. The

141

ponds were lovely in the simple purity of their unspoiled setting. He gulped in astonishment at the scores of ducks that dabbled in the shining waters. It was like looking at a painting.

Through the lad's eyes I too was seeing this gentle scene with fresh awe, joy and enthusiasm. We crouched low in the sagebrush and studied the birds through the binoculars. There were mallards, pintails, widgeon and teal moving across the ponds.

We stood up slowly, hoping to get a closer look.

"They may burst into flight any second!" I murmured softly. "Be ready for a great show!"

Suddenly there was an explosion of wings as scores of birds burst from the surface of the water. The droplets fell from their feet and feathers in a shower of silver rain. The sharp staccato of their wing beats literally filled the sky. Then wave after wave of hurtling bodies swept through the valley just over our heads. They were streaming away in a great circular flight to some other remote waters.

It was all over in moments.
But those brief seconds were charged with energy.
Enthusiasm, eager and ecstatic, welled up within us.
We were touched with the wonder of it all!
Indelible memories had been etched on our minds.

Den turned to me in that special, gentle, happy way of his. "Gee, Grandpa, wasn't that great?!" A look of enormous satisfaction stole over his features. Both of us were richer, much richer, than when we came.

We pushed on past the first pond, and came softly to the edge of the second. There in the soft mud the young bear's tracks were clearly visible in the moist earth. He had prowled all around its perimeter during the night, exploring all the scents and odors of other visitors to this little mountain glen.

I knew where a grand grove of aged firs grew in a cluster. The ground beneath the trees was like a wild park, shaded by the mountain monarchs, cool from the heat of the summer sun. We would go there just "to sit a spell"; to listen to the wind in the tall trees; to wait for some wildlife to wander into this quiet grove.

Den was very still, sensitive to the moods of the hills. He was open in spirit to the impulses of the natural world around us. I assured him in a whisper that we would not have long to wait. So we settled ourselves on a rock outcrop to see what would come.

We had not been there five minutes when there was a

sudden stirring in the lower branches of a dense young pine about forty yards away. We fastened our attention on it. Suddenly an energetic little animal bounded into the tall grass beneath the tree. The tall fronds waved back and forth as it scurried back and forth, coming toward us.

"Don't even blink your eyes, Den," I muttered to my young companion. "Sit as still as a stone!"

We both sat as motionless as petrified rock.
Not a muscle moved.
Not a tendon twitched.
Not a sound escaped us in the mounting tension.

Suddenly a handsome Douglas Squirrel burst out of the grass. With great bounds he began to cross the clearing. Several times he changed direction, leaping over the ground in three-foot jumps that were startling to see.

Closer and closer he came, oblivious that we were even there, sitting still as two stones. The blood raced in my veins. He was so near now I was sure he might even leap right into Den's lap. Instead, he suddenly landed about eighteen inches in front of us. Momentarily he paused there. Somehow we seemed to be neither stones nor stumps.

He riveted us with his sharp eyes. Then he let out a burst of indignation at our intrusion into his terrain. After that he sped away chittering in alarm.

Both of us burst into laughter. What a happy moment. So close, yet so far! But in the brightness of that encounter a sense of beauty, awe and the sheer joy of living shot between us like a charge of electrical energy.

The boy was beyond himself with pure pleasure!

And I, the older one, was being renewed within by the splendor of this day, this golden day.

We stood up, shaking the moss, grass and twigs from our trousers. We were also shaking with gladness and good cheer. This had been an ecstasy shared and in the exuberance I had been brought back to my own boyhood.

Slowly we circled the pond again. Willows and birch and wild rose bushes overhung the far edge of the water. Stealthily we pushed our way through this tangle of dense undergrowth. I half expected to see a skunk or mink or perhaps even a pair of ruffed grouse. Instead I almost stepped on a Blue Racer. This is one of the rarest snakes in our high country. It is a very shy, slender reptile with exquisite blue markings on its slim body.

Den was absolutely captivated by the creature. He had never seen one in his whole life. It rivaled the most beautiful tropical fish in his aquarium at home. Surely we were surrounded with beauty in many forms in these rough mountains.

It was getting late when we finally reached the lake where I had planned for us to have lunch. We found a smooth, moss-covered outcrop of rock on a knoll at the water's edge. There we stretched ourselves in the sun and opened our brown bags. Delicious sandwiches, redolent with ham and cheese and sharp pickle slices, were a meal fit for a monarch.

As we sat munching our food, casting our glances across the sparkling waters of the lake, three black bears suddenly burst out of the trees and rushed up the bank across the little bay from us. At last we had caught up with the little characters whose tracks we had followed all morning.

It was as if a ghost of the imagination had suddenly taken concrete shape in bone, muscle and shining black fur before our eyes. Like three phantoms come to life they hurried across a clearing and vanished into the timber.

For both of us it had been a day of joyous high adventure. The hours had been touched with awe at the unexpected. We had been inspired, stimulated with the wonder

of the world. Fresh enthusiasm had mingled with vivid memories to lend a special splendor to our tramp.

Again I had looked, with warm excitement, through the eyes of a small boy. With the sense of fresh discovery I had tasted the sweet wine of wild berries. In that special sense of well-being, contentment and spontaneous delight of a lad, I again reveled in the flight of birds, the antics of an untamed squirrel, the smooth motion of a jewel-like snake.

Awe, wonder, enthusiasm were being reborn, rekindled, regenerated in an elderly gentleman who hiked in company with a small lad across the high hills against the sky edge.

I am fully confident the same identical sensation swept through the spirit of my Master during those difficult days He tramped the trails of Palestine so long ago. It does not surprise me one bit that He said: "Suffer (let) the little children to come unto me, and forbid them not: for of such is the kingdom of God" (Mark 10:14). He, too, in His time of stress and strain needed the re-quickening which can come from the companionship of a child.

In our age, with a society so jaded with cynicism, so bored with skepticism, what a bright fountain of youth can be found in the heart of a boy or the soul of a girl.

With eyes of wonder they still look out upon a lovely world created with such care by our Father. With souls stirred by awe they find joy in simple, natural life. With spirits of enthusiasm they energize our own. And in it all we can be renewed, if we will!

15

The Shaping of Stone

Smooth stone, shaped and sculptured by natural forces in the high, wild mountain ranges, has always fascinated me. Few are the trips taken along a glacier-fed stream that I do not come home bearing some polished piece of granite, quartz or other rock in my well-worn pockets.

On the rugged stone mantlepiece of our fireplace two very special pieces of worn rock adorn the bright and spacious room. One is a smooth chunk shaped exactly like an ancient Indian tomahawk. Even its cutting edge is sharp as a well-honed knife. Given a wooden handle of tough birch, fastened with deerskin thongs, it could easily serve as a formidable battle-axe to slay an opponent.

The other polished stone is a lovely bit of blue-gray sedimentary rock shaped exactly like a wild mallard's head. It has the same salient facial features complete with a special hole for the eye at precisely the correct spot. Many visitors have been delighted by these stones.

Besides these, for many years we had a large glass jar filled with water, containing a lovely collection of small smooth stones, standing in the kitchen window. Children used to love to look at the smoothly polished pebbles that came in so many delicate colors from rich red to snow white. Each was a little treasure taken from the bed of a swift-flowing mountain stream or gathered from the edge of a sky-blue mountain lake.

There is a rare and unique quality to smooth stones shaped under the impulse of flowing water. The stones speak of long years of wear. Each is a silent tribute to great spans of time during which water was at work on the rock. It tells of patient, quiet subjection to the abrasive forces of the natural world.

Even more stunning and arresting than the small fragments a mountain man can carry home, are the exquisite stream beds carved out of solid rock. Only in the highest streams that have their source at the sky edge may the ultimate beauty of this kind be seen. I say this with all due respect for the magnificent formations found in deep canyons at lower elevations. There, too, the bedrock is often shaped into the most wondrous planes and whorls. But the setting lacks the stupendous magnificence of a mountain backdrop with high snow-spangled peaks pushing into the clouds. There is missing the lure of glaciers thawing in the sun, the melt water from their blue ice charged with "glacial flour" so fine that it forms the most perfect abrasive.

This water, at the eternal verge of freezing, carries in suspension stone worn so fine it hangs suspended in the stream like thin milk. Millennia after millennia the ice-fed freshets flow relentlessly from their mountain source of snow and ice to carve an ever-deepening channel through the upthrust rock formations.

A favorite pastime of mine is to follow one of these highland streams ever upward to its source. The unexpected beauty of the stream bed itself often rivals all the other breathtaking scenery of the country through which the freshet flows. Depending on the type of rock formation, the colors revealed by the running water are of delicate hues. One that is a special favorite cuts through strata of rich red rock interlaced with streaks of brilliant white quartz.

Here the racing water whirls and curls its way over the surface of the stone with sparkling spray and shades of blue and white, reflecting the clear colors of the sky edge. The scene is enchanting.

I love to spend time sitting quietly in meditation beside these mountain streams. Here water has been at work for a very long time indeed. The change from season to season may seem imperceptible. Still the shaping, the smoothing, the sculpting goes on steadily.

Often these little high mountain streams are adorned with the most remarkable trees, shrubs and flowers. At the high altitudes the only trees which can survive are often small and stunted by the stern and rugged weather at the edge of the sky. Beaten down by winter winds, blasted by blizzards bearing tons of snow in their teeth, the little trees take root in some crack of the stone and draw their sustenance from the stream. They resemble bonsai trees, shaped with supreme care to match the elegance of the water-worn streambed.

Here and there a clump of wildflowers will find a sheltered foothold beside the running water. Plants of pioneer species, especially hardy and tough enough to endure the stormy climate of the remote ridges, bloom here in quiet glory. Again and again I have paused in astonishment at the loveliness of Water Willow Herbs, Northern Fireweed and clumps of Mountain Anemone that decorate the verges of these ancient rocks.

In simple truth such spots are the natural "Gardens of God." No man designed them. They were not arranged by human imagination nor brought into being by

our horticultural ingenuity. They are the end product of eons of time during which year upon year ever-increasing loveliness has been brought out of the most unpromising material.

The seeds and spores of ferns and flowers, grass and shrubs, trees and herbs have blown across these ridges on the wind to take root in the rock and gravel. And so out of the most austere setting of ice, snow, gravel and stone there has emerged beauty, elegance and grandeur of divine design.

In the whole realm of outdoor art, there is a profound return to the reality of natural beauty. As a people we are rediscovering the inherent glory of God's creation. We are turning away from the confusion and meaningless expression of abstract art, all of which is a most wholesome trend.

But beyond all this there lies at even greater depths the profound spiritual perceptions which we need to discover as a modern society if we are to survive. Those principles are absolutely basic to any human understanding of what our Father's ultimate objectives are in shaping our lives to His ends.

I for one have become tired of listening to little men with giant self-importance pontificate on the plight of modern man. I am fed up with the flood of books published dealing with the dilemma of our self-centered society. Endless messages are given on the theme of "how people hurt." Amid all this outpouring of self-pity modern man would love to blame God for all that has gone wrong with the world. It is as if He really did not know what He was doing in allowing sorrow and suffering to be so much a part of life.

In my own search for spiritual reality in the midst of so much sadness, my footsteps have been led back again and again to the wonders of the natural world. As with our Master, I find true understanding in such simple things as water, rocks, trees and skies.

This must inevitably be the case. As the supreme Creator is was He who brought the earth into being. It was He who first conceived of things as lovely as sunsets, birds on wing, clouds against the sky or water shaping stone. And it was also He who brought man into being with all his convoluted character.

The principles of creation, re-creation and eternal duration apply equally whether they be in the natural realm of grass and sea and rock or in the supernatural realm of mind and will and stony spirits. This is a salient point which Jesus, the Living Christ, made again and again in His use of simple earthly parables to explain profound spiritual principles. The two realities of natural life and spiritual life are contiguous. They cannot be separated, even though our scholars and theologians would try to deceive us into believing otherwise. Too much, far too much of modern preaching and teaching is based upon purely human philosophy spawned by so-called "thinkers" whose mindset has emerged from the chaos of our man-made urban environment.

And so as I have sought solace and strength and re-assurance for my own soul and spirit in recent months amid the agony of death on every side, I have turned away from the pious platitudes of preachers and teachers and scholars. There was no adequate explanation there for the unending stream of sorrow, the ever-flowing anguish of pain and separation which pours over the planet.

It is not enough to cry out against the agony.
It is not enough to submit sullenly to the sorrow.
It is not enough to accept the separation stoically.

If we are truly Christians, if we are in reality children of the Most High, if we are at all sensitive to God's Gracious Spirit at work in this weary old world, we must be able to perceive our Father's purposes in all our pain.

Is it possible that amid all the mayhem He is actually bringing beauty out of the barrenness of our lives? Is He creating something of consummate loveliness out of our chaos? Is He in fact actually fashioning us to His Own character?

The unequivocal answer is, *"Yes,* He is!"

Somehow we simply must see this!

Again and again as I have sat alone by a singing mountain stream that flowed strongly over the hard bedrock, the acute awareness has come home to my soul. "That, God, is exactly how Your Own eternal, perpetual life flows over me!"

There is a river of divine energy that emerges ever from the very person of the Eternal One. It flows over the entire universe. But more particularly it moves relentlessly over me, around me, as a man. It exerts its influence and power in wondrous ways, some of which may not be even understood or known.

The eternal grace of God manifest in the outpouring of His kindness, compassion, patience and care, whether I deserve it or not, flows fresh and unfailing to me every day. The abundance of His life, His love, His light surround me on every side in joyous effulgence, whether I respond to their stimulation or not. The stirrings of His sweet Spirit surge over my spirit in a dozen ways, carried to me continuously by the constant coming of His presence to bring comfort, consolation and encouragement, whether I am even aware of Him or not.

Across the years and across the tears, He is here!
Ever, always, His quiet assurance is *"I come to you!"*
Our difficulty lies in discerning His presence with us.

It is the constant coming, coming, coming of His life which enables us to understand that thus He truly transcends death. And this life comes to us in many forms and diverse ways that are much more than mere words or vague ideas.

That life comes to us in the integrity of His commitments to us as His people. He carries out His promises. His Spirit does actually bring us comfort. He does console us in the chaos. He does compensate us for our loss.

In the stream of His life that flows to us there may well be the sand and gravel of grievous events that grind us down. But they are the abrasive agents used in His purposes to shape us to His divine design. Just because we are Christians, there are no guarantees given to us by our Father that we shall be exempted or spared from the cutting circumstances of life.

It is often the individuals who have borne the greatest grief and endured the longest abuse who emerge beautiful in character, strong in spirit, unflinching in faith. It is they to whom we turn in our moments of despair. For it is they who have withstood the deep waters of suffering to become lovely in life.

At times, too, the very life of the Living Christ which comes to us may appear to us clouded, maybe even murky. We cannot fully comprehend why the stream of daily events flowing over our little lives resembles the cold, chill glacial streams that bear their burden of "glacial flour." Yet this is the polishing compound that puts the fine polish and smooth satin patina over every stone it touches.

It is the minute pangs of human misunderstandings, the crude, persistent rub of rudeness from others, the little lapses of ingratitude that press in upon us, the subconscious grief of insensitivity that move over us. These are all our Father's "glacial flour" for polishing people in their pangs of pain.

Out of all this there has come to me an acute awareness that nothing is permitted to touch my life except in the gracious good will of my Father for me. In His infinite concern He is shaping a character that not only in time here, but in eternity to come, will reflect something of the wondrous work He did in me.

Out of my stony spirit He has brought something of beauty and worth. It has taken sorrow and suffering. But anything of great value costs a great deal to create and shape.

16

The Splendor in the Clouds

Mountain skies have a grandeur and glory about them rather different from the scenery elsewhere. Because of the higher altitude there is an intimacy and interaction with clouds and mist and storms not often experienced at lower levels.

Instead of observing the various weather systems that pass overhead from far below, in the mountains one is often very much "in the clouds." The high swirling veils of moisture pour through the passes, envelop the high ridges and drape themselves in delicate adornment over the trees and meadows of the high ranges.

We really do live at the sky edge. In the lower valleys the ground, especially in winter, is often bare and brown. But up at our elevation the whole world is wrapped in a wondrous white mantle of shining hoarfrost that sparkles with brilliance under the wide skies of the high mountain ridges.

Some days the moving clouds have deposited such a dense layer of hoarfrost on the trees and shrubs and rocks they appear to be blanketed by snow. But in a couple of hours of intense sunlight, most of the exquisite ice crystals are melted, sheathing every twig, needle and bit of bark in shining dampness.

Up where I live, at the edge of the sky, clouds come and go in a constant forming and dissolution. One hour they may appear to fill the whole inverted bowl of the sky. Then, just as suddenly, the wind may shift direction and the dense cover is torn to fragments that spill out of the sky and vanish into nothing but clear air.

It is much the same with the approach of snow and rain. It is not so much a sensation of feeling these elements are falling on one, as being in the midst of the downfall and watching the flakes or droplets of moisture descend on all sides around one. For anyone who has never lived in high country this may sound absurd but it really is the case.

I shall never forget the first summer showers that came. To the southwest the sky was clear and intensely blue. A strong sun filled the whole valley with brilliant light. Yet immediately around us there were heavy cumulus clouds through which rain was falling in gorgeous silver streams brilliant in the sunlight. It was as if we were at the center of the rain-making action.

This whole sensation becomes ever more spectacular during an electrical storm. All around us there are highly mineralized rock ridges to which the powerful high voltage charges are attracted. The roar of the thunder, the echo of its crashing along the crags, the flash of lightning, the splintering of trees all make for a majestic display of power and glory. Again it is not something happening at a great distance. It is a literal firestorm close at hand.

Some years, if the weather is dry, the lightning strikes

ignite the forests. Great blue-gray clouds of smoke climb into the skies riding the heated updrafts of air. Then the sunrises and sunsets are accentuated with the most vivid colors of orange, red and mauve spread out across the smoky skies.

In winter the snowstorms which envelop us are just as intimate, intense and all-pervasive as the summer showers. There lingers always the peculiar impression: "This is very much a part of my personal life. It is not something remote and apart which is happening. It is here. I am a part of the weather pattern. It is a part of me!"

Often, often, when I go out to hike in the hills, as I attempt to do every day, those moving sentences uttered by the prophet Nahum so long ago come to me with tremendous force. "The Lord hath his way in the whirlwind and in the storm, and the clouds are the dust of his feet" (1:3).

Yes, He is everywhere present. He is everywhere active and at work in the world. Very much alive, He is aware of all that transpires upon the planet and in the lives of its people. Most of us sort of subscribe to this vague idea with mental assent. Precious few people consider the concept important enough to invest their confidence in the omnipresence of Christ. They refuse to have faith in our Father who is actually at work in every event that touches our lives. They do not sincerely believe God's Spirit is everywhere active.

This becomes very obvious in times of great stress or emotional turmoil. It is one of the tragic truths that strikes with great impact when we see men and women surrounded with excruciating sorrow or enveloped in overwhelming grief. It is as if suddenly they feel abandoned by God. In the surging storms of sadness or darkness that sweep over the soul, hope vanishes, faith flees and good will evaporates away.

 Again and again in recent months, since I began to write this book, we have literally been engulfed in storms of sorrow. I wrote in the opening pages that we had shared in the sadness of some fourteen families that faced terminal illness or other tragedies. Since those words were put on the page the number has doubled. One stands in awe at the winds and whirlwinds of grief and agony sweeping over our family and friends.

Just yesterday morning the phone rang. It was the wife of my next dearest friend in this area. Her strong man had suddenly been stricken with a massive stroke. Unable to speak, unable to articulate his thoughts, unable to move one side of his big sturdy frame, he now lay like a fallen tree.

This was the twenty-ninth person in our circle of friends to have the terrible threat of death descend like a dark cloud across the horizon of life. In eighteen months the tragic sort of story had swept over us in agonizing intensity almost thirty times. O the tears, the fears, the inner anguish!

Again and again, the stabbing, searing, searching questions come through trembling lips and tear-burned eyes: "Can God be in all of this? Is He really here? Does He truly care?"

In such moments pious platitudes will not do!
We cannot mumble sweet nothings!
There can be no vague ideas!

The excruciating crisis demands formidable faith in the Living Christ. It calls for unshakable confidence in the love of our Father. It must have the consolation and assurance of God's gracious Spirit.

"Yes!" Again and again I affirm the truth. "He has His way in the whirlwind and in the storm. The clouds are the dust of His feet." He, the Risen One, the Living God, is here present in our pain. He is at work in the whirlwind of our despair, moving behind the scenes in the dark clouds of our chaos and confusion.

Only He will or can bring beauty out of it all. Only He can bring help to our helplessness. Only He can restore joy for our sorrow. There is no other word of consolation or cheer that I can bring to those in dark places.

It may well be asked, how can you be so sure? My simple reply as a humble lay person is based upon three indisputable aspects of life. The first is the inviolate truth of our Father's Own Word to us as His people. Untold millions of individuals in their hour of sorrow have found faith and courage and calm strength coming to them from God in the midst of the storm.

Secondly, there has been my own private, moving discovery across the long years of my life that I am never alone in the times of trial. Christ has always been there in the turmoil of excruciating events which appear to be so threatening. Mary, who on the resurrection morning could not clearly recognize her Master through tear-stained eyes and could not comprehend His living Presence in the midst of death, exclaimed, "*Rabboni.*" Then He softly spoke her name. So I have seen Him dimly, but alive!

Thirdly, there is the subsequent result of all the storms and clouds and wild winds that sweep about us. At the hour they seem so tempestuous. But at a later date their benefits are clearly seen.

For out of the rain, out of the sleet, out of the snow, out of the storms there comes to the high country the cleansing, the refreshment, the moisture, the sustenance that eventually renews the mountains. Here in truth new beauty is born that adorns the high ridges with a mantle of shining white. Out of the stormy weather spills moisture that refreshes the alpine meadows, the lofty forests and sky edge rangelands.

Only because of clouds and mists and surging storms does moisture percolate through the soil to feed the mountain springs, to enliven the upland streams, to replenish the roaring rivers and fill the lakes anew.

Out of what appears to be death, new life emerges.

When today there is turmoil, stress and darkness, tomorrow new fields of flowers will flourish on the slopes.

In the skies so laden with heavy overcast, so charged with clouds and wind-driven snow this week, birds will soar on wing against the sun next spring. For this, too, will pass. The skies will be blue again.

All is change. Life is ever in flux. Nothing on earth remains constant. But in splendor and wonder those of us who know Christ shout with glad affirmation, *"O God, Thou changest not!"* Amid the mayhem in calm confidence we assert boldly, *"Forever, O Lord, Thou art faithful."*

A small parable illustrating this truth so forcibly was given to me as a gift by my wife on a handsome bookmark. It came home to my heart with remarkable clarity the morning I first read it. Since the author is unknown I share it here with the reader, written as concisely as possible in my own words.

The parable is entitled "Footprints."

A man, near the end of his life, looked back to see all the events of his years played out before him again in rapid succession. He seemed to be strolling along the sand with the drama of his days being enacted on a giant screen against the sky edge.

He noticed that wherever he walked there were two sets of parallel footprints left upon the sand—his own and those of his Master, the Lord Christ.

As the drama of his days unfolded something else struck him forcibly. Whenever he passed through some very dark experience or there was a time of unusual sorrow or hardship, there was only one set of footprints.

Turning to the Lord he asked, "O Lord, You promised never to leave me! How is it there is only one set of footprints when the going was so rough?"

In tenderness and love the Master looked at him and replied: *"You did not know it. But it was then I carried you!"*

In essence that is the splendor, the glory, the majesty of the very love of God present in the storms of life. He is ever present with His people even in the darkest hour. It is He who carries us through. And on the other side we look back in retrospect to see His faithfulness every day, all the way, whatever men may say.

Clouds come and go. He remains constant.

Winds blow, storms subside. He is ever by our side.

Out of it all, He alone brings comfort, consolation and the great renewal which is such abundant compensation for all the crushing sorrow of our years—and the burning agony of our tears.

He, and He alone, makes all things new—both in this life and in the wider life yet to come beyond the skies. Bless His wondrous name forever and forever!

17

Hidden Springs

Earlier in this book it was mentioned that unlike many mountain regions, ours is dry terrain, almost arid in nature. On average, in any given year, less than twelve inches of moisture fall on this high country. This includes the winter snowpack. So in truth it almost approaches desert country.

For this reason springs, streams and mountain lakes are here considered jewels of great worth to be treasured. Without them these beautiful ranges that reach ever upward to the sky edge would be almost barren of life and destitute of vegetation.

Because I am an ardent outdoorsman with a fond affection for all things wild and natural, springs of water have always fascinated me. They are a vital source of life for trees, shrubs, grass, flowers, mammals, birds, livestock and even man. This was especially true in pioneer days when frontiersmen did not have use of modern power equipment with which to sink deep wells that could tap the subterranean water supplies. Then the hidden natural springs were rare treasures of great worth. To a certain degree they still are in our rugged mountains where it is not always possible to get in with power equipment.

In the long years of my mountain adventures I have drunk from scores of upland springs. The clear, cool water, free of any impurities, uncontaminated by man or his chemicals, is the sweetest drink available on the planet. Here the bears, the deer, the squirrels, the birds, the butterflies and other uncounted life forms come to slake their thirst. For they, too, know the hidden springs. From the free-flowing liquid they draw life and sustenance in the desert heat of summer and chilling frost of winter.

Yes, even in winter the springs still flow freely. The water emerging from beneath the mountain slopes remains at an almost constant temperature, melting away the accumulating snow and ice that forms a small basin around them.

Because I have always found special pleasure in discovering where the hidden springs are in the hills, there has been a double delight in clearing them of dirt and debris which is bound to accumulate across the years. Deer, elk, wild sheep or domestic range cattle often trample the source of the spring. Rock and fallen earth may fall into the flow and almost shut it off. Broken branches or fallen leaves from the surrounding trees and shrubs that always encircle these lovely spots will often fill them with debris.

So I take the time to clear away the accumulation of decaying material. Sometimes it takes a sturdy effort to lift the rocks, stones and mud that block the flow. But the pure pleasure of seeing the mountain-fed water surge out strongly is a sensation of sweet satisfaction. I often enclose a small space with rocks that form a natural basin where all forms of wildlife can drink with ease and pleasure.

Here all my friends of hoof, wing and paw can come to refresh themselves. Here the game trails converge. Here the birds come swiftly and silently to assuage their thirst and freshen their plumage.

The water springs are also a special place where certain unique types of vegetation flourish. Because of crystal clear water that remains at an even temperature, watercress thrives in these spots. Not only do the deer and bears relish this delicacy, but so do I. Bunches of the herb are borne home for delectable sandwiches.

It is around the hidden springs in the hills that Red Osier Dogwood thrives. It is a magnificent water-loving shrub whose lacework branches form dense thickets around the springs. In spring they are brilliant green. In summer they are adorned with dense clusters of white berries that bears relish and on which birds gorge with pleasure. In fall the foliage turns crimson, filling the deep rock draws with red and purple hues.

Here, too, the native Hawthorn takes root. The sturdy little trees with their scarlet berries, shiny leaves and labyrinth of thorny branches are beloved of birds. Almost every mature "haw, haw" tree shelters at least one bird's nest. Nor is it possible to find their secret shelter until winter winds have stripped away the last gold and scarlet leaves.

The hidden springs are special spots of unusual beauty. In more open locations they are often encircled with a green sward of grass. I love to lie here in the sun and listen to the soft sounds of the clear water running between the rocks. Often the surrounding stones are sheathed in deep soft moss. Ferns and flowers grow among the rocks and nature shapes a bit of pristine paradise in this spot.

What is the secret of the hidden springs? How is it possible for so much life and vigor and beauty to be sustained in these austere surroundings? Whence the clear, pure-flowing streamlet that turns a waste of rock and sand and blasted mountain slope into a vale of refreshment?

The source lies in the great skies that arch over the lofty, shining peaks. It is the weather systems of cloud and mist and snow and rain that swathe these heights in veils of moisture. It is the shining snowfields on the summit of the ranges and crest of the high ridges. It is the gentle, persistent percolation of moisture through rock and soil and forest duff to emerge in this spot.

The mountain spring is not its own source of origin. Its story does not begin where it is born and come to light in the shining sun. The energy of its flow, the quickening of its waters are not inherent in the spring itself. Rather, the spring, amid so much desolation and desert dryness, gives life from a source outside itself, of eternal duration far beyond its own tiny boundaries.

The hidden springs high in the hills at the edge of the sky are an intimate, quiet, gentle expression of the eternal elements of the universe. Here compressed into a tiny stream of life-giving liquid lies a tiny fragment of the titanic forces of wind and weather that encircle the planet to determine its climate. These are the elemental sources of energy derived from sun, moon, stars and all the awesome arrangements ordained of God our Father in creation of the cosmos.

Often, in quiet solitude, I have reflected on such truths as I drank from a spring, then sat down gently to listen to its eternal music.

In utter sincerity, with soul-searching humility of spirit, I have asked myself, "Could my little life possibly be one of God's hidden springs in the wasteland of our world?" It is a perfectly legitimate and appropriate question. "Does there really flow out of my innermost being and through my person the pure, living water of the very life of the Living Christ?" These are sobering reflections. They call for honest answers in a culture that is as crude as a barren desert, a society as barren of belief as a rock slope. "Can men and women around me, jaded with sorrow, wrung out with pain, dry and bitter with remorse, find refreshment and new quickening in my company?"

When our Master walked among us He stated emphatically that it could be so. Just as He renewed and refreshed those who came to Him to drink of His life, so He declared the same could be true of us. But unlike Him, our source is not in ourselves. The vitality, the energy, the dynamic, the beauty, the renewal which emanates from me has its source in Him. Otherwise, it can never, ever, satisfy the thirsting soul.

The flow of life surging and pulsing through me to refresh this weary old world must be from God Himself. It must be the continuous out-pouring of His Presence by His Spirit which touches and transforms all around me. Any person naïve enough, arrogant enough, stupid enough to believe that it is his or her own charm, charisma or capabilities that change and enliven others, lives in utter self-delusion.

One of the terrible tragedies of human behavior is for people to turn to other human beings in an effort to find sustenance for their spirits. They are always deluded, ever disappointed. Our spirits can only find life in the Living Spirit of the Living Lord. Our eternal quest for life-giving water can only be quenched by the eternal life of God Himself coming to us through the hidden springs of His own person who indwells those who are open channels for His life.

The best of us have lives that, like the mountain springs, are often plugged with debris and muddied with fallen earth and rock. The supply of live water is almost cut off because of the trampling of hooves, the accumulation of dead wood and leaves.

Most of us as God's people are really not vibrant springs through which there surges the very life of the eternal God. The hard knocks of life, the rocks of rank unbelief, the mud of trampled hopes and broken dreams, the silt of sorrow and sadness, the dead wood of death and despair, the fallen leaves of frustration often choke off Christ's life in us.

People come to us searching for strength, uplift, solace and refreshment. Instead, they find despair, defeat and dark bitterness. Too often our characters are choked up with the cares of life, the calamities of our corrupt society, the ennui of a cynical culture. We claim to be Christians, the children of the Most High, when in reality we are a reproach to our Father, a despair to His Spirit.

What we need, and need desperately, is to be renewed ourselves. We need a sudden cleansing, pulsing surge of God's Own Life to flush away the debris. We need His grace to scour away the silt and mud of a wrong mindset, to flow freely through us without hindrance.

As men and women search us out in the dry and barren hills of our times they will discover a quiet, gentle, hidden spring through which there pulses the very life of Christ. It is of Him they must drink, not of us! It is of His life and energy they must imbibe, not of our human personality. It is by His vitality they will be quickened, made alive, fully refreshed, not by our fallible human nature.

Jesus was very explicit when He stated categorically, "He that believeth on me, as the scripture hath said, out of his innermost being shall flow rivers of living water!" (John 7:38). To believe in Christ is to open one's life to Him completely. It is actually to allow Him unobstructed access into our souls and spirits. It is literally to permit Him to fill us with His presence. It is to take of His very life and imbibe of it fully. It is utterly to assimilate Him until our whole being is saturated, revitalized and overflowing with His life.

When this takes place we become the hidden springs through which the renewal and refreshment of God's very life flows to others. He it is, then, who touches and transforms all around us. It is He who brings life out of death, love out of despair and His joy out of our mourning.

18

Quiet Waters

All of us need to find some quiet waters in life. Like the oasis for the caravan crossing the sun-scorched desert, so still waters are for the soul seared by the anguish of sorrow. There need to be moments of respite when in utter tranquillity of spirit our Father can be given opportunity to speak to us softly to renew our spirits.

Such times often come to me in the gentle company of high mountain lakes. These small sheets of shining water are cupped in the hills, sometimes surrounded by delicate stands of birch, poplar and willow. Others, above timber line, stand stark against the sky edge rimmed by rock and a few hardy reeds, tough enough to endure the environment of the high altitude.

The beauty and serenity of these still waters is duplicated by the incredible reflections mirrored in their shining surface. Every tree, snag, rock, distant ridge, soaring mountain peak and fluffy cloud suspended in the sky are reproduced as by a miracle in the gleaming water.

Here not a breath of air stirs the surface or wrinkles the water. It is as smooth as polished pewter. Sometimes on very chill mornings after a clear night of extreme cold the lake will be locked in a sheet of glare ice which serves equally as a perfect mirror.

When autumn colors flame in the trees, and early frost has burnished the lake or marsh edge with tints of bronze and copper, the total effect is one of majestic splendor. It is as if a painting of huge proportions has been executed on the landscape by *a master artist*.

That, in fact, is exactly what has been done. For it was our Father who initially designed such loveliness to adorn the earth. And all subsequent art forms have found their inspiration at this source.

For the soul sensitive to the uplift of quiet waters there come moments, breathless moments, when in truth the whole earth speaks in hushed tones: *"O God, You are here! Your presence fills this place! Your peace enfolds these skies."*

And because He is there, my spirit, too, attuned to His, can find refreshment, renewal and restoration in such a spot. This is not to indulge in some spurious imagination of the mind. Rather, it is to discover the wholesome healing of the entire person in the presence of the Most High.

This element of utter serenity, of complete stillness, of lovely tranquillity in company with Christ, is a dimension of life that increasingly eludes us Americans. It is not that millions of us do not crave it. But it is unfortunately ever more difficult to find. The simple reason is that more and more multitudes are imprisoning themselves in large metropolitan centers where the roar and rumble of industry, traffic and commerce never cease.

Added to this is the insistence of modern man that wherever he goes, even into the countryside and remaining wilderness areas, he must take his twentieth-century gadgetry with him. The thunder of all-terrain vehicles, the drone of aircraft, the scream of snowmobiles or power boats, the staccato rattle of dirt bikes all shatter the stillness and desecrate the solitude of those who seek it.

Nevertheless all is not lost. Here and there stretches of unspoiled terrain remain. For those who will take the time and make the effort, quiet spots can still be found where serene waters bask in the sun and reflect the gentle glory of the sky edge.

There is one such spot just a few miles from my hearth. Tucked away between brown rock bluffs of very ancient lava these waters have somehow, as by a miracle, escaped the intrusion of modern man. Not once have I ever found an empty can or paper wrapping around their edge.

Whenever I come, I find a special tranquillity that defies description in common language. There is an element of profound peace that immediately permeates the awareness of anyone who enters the area with hushed steps. Loud language and coarse conversation are simply not acceptable. Human sounds are an intrusion. Crude use of any mechanical device would be a desecration.

I often go there simply to sit, to observe the scene, to think deep thoughts, to meditate over the meaning of life, to ask profound questions, to commune with Christ in the depths of my spirit.

These still waters are not a place of stagnation. Quite the opposite, they serve as a powerful magnet that attracts a startling array of wildlife. Their moisture provides a rich environment for all sorts of vegetation that lends lovely diversion to the dry arid region.

Here ducks dabble in the shallows. More often, they simply rest on the surface, looking almost like carved decoys reposing on a glass tabletop, their smooth shapes reflected to perfection in the surface. A heron will often stand as still as a miniature statue carved in stone, waiting at the water's edge for a careless bit of prey to come his way.

Overhead, cumulus clouds drift softly across the sky. Their white forms are caught in duplicate by the water. Like billowing white sails on the sea they drift slowly across the lake in steady procession. The blue skies and white clouds adorning the scene in exquisite patterns of pristine beauty add tremendous breadth to the scene.

Momentarily there is a splash at the water's edge. A muskrat moves out of the reeds that rim the shore. He swims across the water, fracturing its mirror surface into fragments of what may appear as broken glass. Then suddenly he stops. The ripples soon subside. And once again all is still as he lies there like a brown stone, soaking up the warmth of the morning sun.

A pair of swallows, graceful in flight, swift on wing, swoop over the quiet waters with splendid smoothness. Their acrobatics, so silent, so smooth, so swift, actually accentuate the quietude. Here amid such solitude they glean their harvest of insects without disturbing the stillness of the spot.

A fringe of graceful reeds encircles the little lakes. Their slim foliage forms a delicate pattern of basketlike weaving in the water. Intertwined and criss-crossed by the breeze, it is as if they had been interwoven by the wind.

Here and there a Red-Winged Blackbird makes his music amid their shafts. The mellow notes rippling across the little valley with purity and a touch of the wild on their edge, remind me that Red-Wings have come to this place of peace for a thousand years.

A Whitetail Doe steps out of the dim shadows of the Black Birches on the bank. Because I sit so still she has not spotted me. No stray eddy of air bears my scent to her twitching nostrils. Step by step, in silent but deliberate action, she moves into the strong sunlight. A fawn follows her. His spotted coat glistens gold and white in the bright light. Both doe and fawn dip their black muzzles in the cool waters. Only briefly do they pause to refresh their lips and throats. Then softly they turn away and step back into the dim, dark shadows of the trees.

It is an instant of delight—a scene of supreme serenity. It is a moment of joy, an uplift of the spirit. All of it is unplanned; none of it is arranged by man. It is a pure but gentle gift from God. In our common lives such simple incidents come as treasures beyond calculation. They are cameos of beauty, healing, love and restoration that remain etched on the memory, never to be erased.

These incidents endure while all around time erases other events. The passing of the hours wipes away other transient concerns.

The joyous renewal that comes to the anguished soul in solitude assures me again and again of my Father's care that enfolds His earth children. If we are to know His compassion, if we are to sense His touch upon our torn spirits, if we are to feel the caress of His hand upon our wounded hearts, we must seek Him in solitude.

It is no accident that His Spirit speaks to us with such clear perception as the psalmist wrote: *"Be still and know that I am God . . . . I will be exalted in the earth"* (Psalm 46:10).

We modern people live so much amid turmoil, tension

and the trauma of a fractured world. So, when death strikes or illness of terminal nature tears away the fragile fabric of one's thin veneer of invulnerability, most men and women know not where to turn for shelter. It is as if they stand exposed, naked, stripped and shattered by the suffering and sorrow that has swept over them in a whirlwind of horror.

Again and again I have been through the storms of suffering with other human beings who really wondered if there would or could be a way out. Was there a place of peace? Was there some spot of stillness for the soul?

My answer over and over is, "Yes!" But one must search, and seek, and find it in the presence of Jesus Christ, who is from everlasting to everlasting, who changes not across the centuries, who is eternal, Creator of heaven and earth, yet also Creator of my complex character.

We cannot find such assurance in the mayhem and madness of our great commercial complexes. Nor will we ever find it in the sophisticated skepticism of science and technology. Nor will it be found in our most august academic intellectualism. None of these philosophies can ever mend the soul torn with sorrow or the spirit seared with suffering. They are all cold, clinical and cruel!

But we can find renewal in the stillness of a lake; the drift of clouds against the sky edge; the flight of a bird across the water; the reflection of a deer coming to drink; the limpid, liquid notes of a blackbird in the reeds. These things have been ever of old. They are as ancient as the duration of days. They speak impressively of eternal values. They remind us that our Father is ever here, nor does He change.

In their constancy we see reflected something of His continuing care and compassion for us. We comprehend, even if only dimly, in the beauty of grass and trees and sky and sun, a little of the glory and wonder of our God who continually makes all things new. In our innermost beings we grasp again the enduring truth that if He can sustain all the earth in its pristine splendor from generation to generation, He can sustain our souls as well. It is He and He alone who can regenerate us in spirit both in this life now and in that to come.

In essence to *know Him* is *to know life eternal!*
This is that which surpasses our suffering.
It is this which overcomes even death.
So we are set free from all fear.
All is well. He is here.
Thank You, Father!

19

Return of the Birds

As I write these words the worst of winter is over. Though last night the temperature hovered down around zero, and the trees stood stiff and stark in the bitter cold, there is a change in the weather. Each day the sun is a little higher in the sky, a few more degrees above the sky edge. Its warmth increases steadily. Here and there on the south slopes there is a snow melt with brown earth and green grass showing between the white drifts.

Yesterday I took a long tramp in the brilliant, late winter sunshine. And though I have welcomed scores of springs in the north, it excited me again to notice the return of the birds. I had scarcely left the front door when a great black raven, shining like a polished boot, tumbled through the high cold air in glad abandon. His raucous cries rang across the ridges and came slanting down the airwaves to me. Already he was making his wild mating call.

Even more dramatic was a magnificent Golden Eagle soaring sedately above the great ragged firs on the sky line above our chalet. With powerful precision this monarch of the mountain winds etched perfect circles against the sky edge. Often I have stood spellbound watching a ragged band of crows try to mob one of these regal birds. With screams of outrage and cries of alarm they dive at the eagle which only turns its rapier beak or displays its fierce talons to send them off in terror.

Sailing serenely to some gnarled old crag on a rock ridge, the eagle will alight with dignity. Then composing itself in quiet strength it will sit calmly until the last of the crows exhausts its empty tirades and flies away in utter frustration. Then once again peace prevails.

As I hiked along the edge of a frozen streambed a small flock of my favorite chickadees called and fluttered through the undergrowth. Where the warming sun had bared the soil, they dropped to the ground and scratched busily among the decaying leaves. They are always harbingers of good cheer and better things to come, even when they work their way through the pine needles just outside our large patio windows. There the wind rocks them gently as they search for forage in the whispering foliage.

Always seeming so full of energy and joyous vitality, they did not appear the least concerned about what crisis tomorrow might bring. They had sufficient for this day. That was enough to cheer about.

Further on down the valley I heard the distant call of a Downy Woodpecker. This was another sure sign that soon all the woods and hills would ring with the songs of birds. I followed the sounds of his cry and saw his flight across some open ground to a grove of white-barked Aspens shining in the sun.

He was searching for stalks of dry Mullen. The ragged brown plants appear so dead, so inert, so utterly useless. But locked tight in those shaggy stalks is a virtual banquet for the birds. And long ago the dainty little woodpeckers learned how to unlock the rich store of delicacies for their own survival in the spring.

I went on down the sun-drenched valley even further. It startled me to see that in some of the more sheltered spots all the snow was gone. Brown earth, sun-bleached grass from last year, gray rocks and sage were the muted tones that covered the landscape. But despite their apparent drabness all spoke eloquently of a long winter that was past and a new spring about to begin.

In the far distance there came that ecstatic sound of wild geese on the wing—not the high wild notes of a great wedge of the giant birds going to the arctic. This was the much more intimate "goose gabble" of a flock in search of local nesting grounds. These were the fore-fliers who came early from nearby open waters to find a marsh or open stream or even gentle spring which might lend itself as a home for a goose colony.

The strong birds straggled through the valley in a loose and untidy formation. Their excited calls were those of mating pairs surveying the land below for suitable homesteads. They had been this way before. It was familiar terrain. Still they searched it carefully for a suitable spot to set down and stay for the summer.

Yes, the birds were back. Their presence was a sure sign that winter was over. The dark days were gone; the long, dreary nights were behind. Each week it would become warmer. Every new day would be a little brighter. Each dawn held vivid promise of better things to come.

Contemplating all this it came home to me with formidable force that really it was all a precise replay of the recent, spiritual experiences we had passed through. There had been chilling days of sharp anxiety for those who faced death. We had known dark hours of sorrow for those who had bade loved ones farewell. There had been the grim vigil of those who endured the unknown future alone. All of these were akin to winter in the soul and night in the spirit.

Sometimes it seemed the long nights far, far outstretched the brief days. Despair and darkness far, far outweighed the brief interludes of hope and cheer. The forlorn fears were far worse than the bright promises of renewal.

Yet behind the scenes of sorrowing, pain and acute suffering our Father was still very much at work in the weariness of our winter. His faithfulness to His people would prevail over and beyond all the agony of their human despair. His concern and His care would change the impossible anguish into new and fresh opportunities to begin again.

That is how it was every spring.
That is how it was with Him.
The birds were back.
Hope came anew at the sky edge.

Here and there like a solitary rascal of a raven tumbling gleefully in the wind, a sudden spectacle of fun and good cheer would tumble through our thoughts. Borne on the wind of God's powerful Spirit some joyous word of encouragement or little experience of ecstatic delight would sweep into life to dispel a bit of the gloom.

There were hours, yes, sometimes even days or maybe weeks, when the crows of craven fear and apprehension seemed to crowd in upon us. The ragged cries of cowardice and black regret seemed to gang up on us. But we found a place of peace, a spot of strength as we settled down quietly to be still and know the presence of the Living Christ who abides with us always. Eventually the harassments of the opposition would fade away and we would know the rest of those who trust in God.

Some of the most unpromising circumstances became suddenly brighter when like the chickadees, they were invaded by unexpected bits of light. It astonished me to see how one unexpected knock at the door, a letter from a long-forgotten associate, a bit of fun with a friend, a hilarious cameo of humor could come winging into the day to drive away the despair.

There were a dozen ways in which our Father arranged for "birds of joy" to return, bringing with them hope and healing for the deep hurts of my wounded heart. In His mercy, love and compassion He had ways of bringing light and love back into the gloom.

Beyond this there were those quiet interludes when like the woodpecker, searching for the Mullen plants, I found a hidden banquet in the pages of God's own promises to me as His child. There was life and there was spirit imbedded in my Father's word for me. Where before it seemed death was so dominant, now suddenly vital life sprang up anew. Where previously despair prevailed, now, radically, incredible love came to my soul. Where in the winter of my darkness there was such a long night, now in wonder and joy the brightness of new light and hope came alive.

Nor were these just passing whimsies or transient sensations that would delude and discourage those of us who passed through the dark shadows of the valley of death. They were much more permanent and enduring than that. Like the straggling skeins of great winged geese searching for a spot to nest, so the coming of Christ's Gracious Spirit, the Comforter, had arrived to take up permanent residence in the labyrinth of my life.

With fresh awareness and acute intensity there swept over my spirit those ancient, unshakable, marvelous words of old:

> *"Be strong and of a good courage;*
> *be not afraid, neither be thou dismayed;*
> *for the Lord thy God is with thee whithersoever*
> *thou goest"* (Joshua 1:9).

There, in essence, was the secret to renewal. The presence of the Most High would enable me and my friends to surmount every sorrow. He it was who would bring spring to the soul again. Because of His great faithfulness joy would come once more to the spirit.

20

The Wonder
of Spring

Only the person who has spent a severe winter in a northern latitude, at comparatively high altitudes, will ever fully
comprehend the true wonder of spring. There really is no
other physical experience on the planet which can quite
match the magic of the melting of the snow. Nothing is so
designed to stimulate the entire body and quicken all the
senses as the return of warm weather, stronger sunlight
and renewal of the earth.

As adaptable as man may be, the long winter nights,
the deep freeze of unrelenting cold, the unmerciful winds
bearing blizzards, tend to shrink one's soul and shrivel the
spirit as if constricted in a prison. It is the coming of spring
that sets one free. The gentle advent of strong, warm sunshine liberates one's locked-in life to wander at will once
more.

This explains why ancient tribes of the north could
not help but adore the return of spring. There is an aura of

awe and worship in seeing green grass spring up anew from beneath the snowbanks. Strong men will sometimes fall down upon all fours to kiss the sun-warmed soil that has lain locked in frost for months. The tinkle of snow melting from glasslike icicles, the sweet singing of streams flowing free again, the ever-widening circle of bare ground around every tree trunk—all are powerful impulses that purge the soul of its dark reflections, giving glorious hope to the heart and new songs to the soaring spirit.

The final triumphant display of new life is the joyous return of the birds accompanied by the stirring resurrection of fresh foliage adorning the land. Turgid buds swell and burst into tender new leaves. Bare twigs and branches of willow, birch, poplar and a hundred lesser shrubs are dressed in glowing greenery. New grass and a thousand varied wildflowers push new shoots from the sun-warmed soil. Spring has come!

In our western mountains and desert valleys some four thousand diverse species of wildflowers carpet the countryside. In frontier days, before the advent of the pioneer's plow and the range rider's hordes of "hooved locusts," the earth glowed with the glory of fields of flowers. The display now is much less dramatic, much more subdued, altered by the invasion of cheat-grass, gray sage, knapweed and other noxious plants.

Still for those of us who search out the secluded valleys and climb the steepest slopes there are spots where the upland flower fields are a majestic spectacle. In some areas hundreds of acres are blanketed in blossoms of every possible hue. Whole ridges are alive with masses of blooms too beautiful to describe with mere words.

Where there was barrenness suddenly there is exquisite beauty. Where the mountains against the sky edge were a stark white, now they are dressed in vivid green, yellow, red and white flowers. Where there had been utter severity of scenery, now suddenly there has come softness and splendor as if painted with an artist's brush.

This total transformation of the high country from winter to spring dress remains one of the most magnificent spectacles upon the planet. The total transfiguration is a moving panorama that progresses with enormous power and perfect precision. It is governed by the celestial movement of the sun, moon, stars and planets, all in orbits ordained by the meticulous mind of our Father God.

There is nothing haphazard about spring. It is not a fickle affair that happens some years and not others. Its advent is sure; its impact is enormous. Its coming produces incredible changes. It ushers in a wondrous re-generation of life.

For those of us sensitive in soul to the changes around us, spring spells liberty, freedom and stimulation. Our spirits, attuned to the world around us, surge with new life. The urge to go out and explore, to hike, to climb a cliff, to roam at random, to wander free in the wind is a heady impulse that cannot be denied. Our hearts are set to singing. A bright light of excitement fills our eyes. Our muscles must move. Our strength must be spent in splendid exhilaration.

Though we scarcely seem to realize it, we too are being re-made, quickened, reborn in resurrection life. The winter is past, the darkness is gone, the cold has vanished under the warming sun. And we are free, free, free! No wonder we want to walk for miles, to climb a hill, to laugh in the sun, to sing in the breezes that blow so softly, to throw off our jackets and bare our faces to the touch of spring.

Everywhere there is new life. The zest of renewal reassures us: all will be well. The coming of April flowers, the refreshment of spring showers, the sheer loveliness of shining cumulus clouds towering high against the sky edge relaxes our pent-up bodies. We rejoice in the wonder of it

all. Somehow, suddenly, we are at rest. An ancient saying
suggests, "Our God is in His heaven, and all is at peace on
earth."

But all of this takes time and thought and quiet moments to enjoy. Primitive people with long outdoor traditions fully understood the uplift and inspiration that came
to them from gentle contemplation of the cosmos. It is an
ancient aspect of life that has been pretty well lost in the
madness of our modern society. Few indeed are those people of our generation who know anything at all about moments of meditation in which Christ can be given a chance
to commune with them in the depths of their spirits.

The reader of this book may not have realized that its
chapters have actually led step by step through the four
seasons of the year. Unlike most such works, it began with
the high noon of summer and now ends with the surge of
spring. This was done deliberately to portray the parallels
of our common human spiritual pilgrimage.

We begin our life with God in a strong and buoyant
season, sometimes called our "first love." But it is usually
followed by the subdued events of a fall season during
which a much more mellow mood engulfs our souls. Then
come those severe storms of sorrow, the tough trials of
pain and parting, the winter winds of adversity. Our faith
is tested. Our confidence in Christ is constricted. But as
we endure, spring comes again. We are renewed. The
truth and credibility of Christ's resurrection power engulfs us. We are assured of His everlasting hope and life.
Love springs anew within our spirits. Faith flames bright
again. All is well, for *He is here!*

The great cycle of the seasons goes on year upon year,
enacted against the giant backdrop of the sky edge. We
watch in humble awe and spellbound wonder as moon after moon the pageantry of the planet is played out upon
the earth. The sublimely orchestrated script of the Divine
Director is acted out in incredible detail by ten thousand

participants. Each is directed by His will, guided by His genesis, moved by His inspiration.

If this can be true for lesser life forms, such as birds and bees and bears and Balsam Root or Bunch Grass, then surely it can be equally true for us human beings created in Christ's own image. The utter tragedy and terrible truth is it seldom does happen. For horror upon horror, most men's hearts (wills) have been deliberately set, and very purposely hardened, against the gracious good will of our loving Father.

This need not be so. There can be harmony between us and Him. It is not impossible for a person to come to *truly know Christ,* whom to know is life everlasting. It is absolutely true that if men and women welcome Christ as wholeheartedly as they welcome the warmth of spring, new life, abundant life, the very life of the risen Lord, can pour into their beings.

It is this total availability of a soul to the impinging presence of the Living Lord that can set them free. Just as the sun of spring rising ever higher in the sky releases the earth from its winter bondage, so the new life of the Risen Sun, the Christ of God, sets our spirits free. Jesus, Himself, said without apology, "If the Son (Sun) therefore shall make you free, ye shall be free indeed" (John 8:36). Free to follow Him. Free to revel in His love. Free to find abundant energy, hope and life in Him.

All of us have our summer days of strength and bright assurance. All of us, too, have our autumn days when the shadows lengthen across our years. All of us will have our winters of deep despair and the dark pain of death. And all of us can know again the powerful resurgence of Christ's triumphant, overcoming life made real in our experience by His presence and resurrection power.

This book has been an impassioned plea for men and women to find their life, their strength, their love, their hope, their ultimate healing and wholeness in Christ. All other human philosophies will cheat us of the best. All other false religions, mysticism or spiritism of any sort, are but a delusion that leads to darkness, despair and death.

But glory of glories, wonder of wonders, Christ brings His light amid our darkness. He brings His love into our despair. He brings His life to replace our death. *He is springtime to our souls!*

W. PHILLIP KELLER was born in East Africa and trained as an agronomist. He has worked as an agricultural development specialist, wildlife photographer and naturalist, and has expressed his love for nature and its God in many bestsellers. *Sky Edge* is his thirty-fourth book. Among his bestselling books are *A Gardener Looks at the Fruits of the Spirit, Wonder O' the Wind* (his autobiography), *Lessons from a Sheepdog* (also on film and cassette), and *A Shepherd Looks at Psalm 23.* He is a popular author, lecturer, photographer, lay speaker, agrologist and ecology consultant. Keller is a graduate of the University of Toronto and Brooks Institute of Photography in California. His writing emanates from personal in-depth study of God's Word, intense prayerful meditation, and the sharing of spiritual truth with groups of God's people in various countries. In addition to books, he is featured on such Life-Lifter cassettes as "Forgiveness—What It Is and What It Costs," "The Potter and the Clay," and "What It Means to Receive Christ."